protection

An ALNAP guide for humanitarian agencies

Hugo Slim | Andrew Bonwick

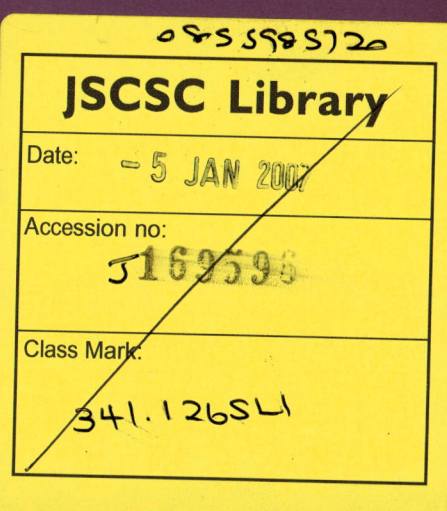

The first printing of this book was published in August 2005 by ALNAP and distributed by
the Overseas Development Institute under the ODI ISBN (0 85003 762 X).
The first (February 2006) and subsequent reprints are distributed for ALNAP by Oxfam Publishing
under the Oxfam ISBN (0 85598 572 0).
A catalogue record for this publication is available from the British Library.

Available from:
Bournemouth English Book Centre, PO Box 1496, Parkstone, Dorset, BH12 3YD, UK
tel: +44 (0)1202 712933; fax: +44 (0)1202 712930; email: oxfam@bebc.co.uk

USA: Stylus Publishing LLC, PO Box 605, Herndon, VA 20172-0605, USA
tel: +1 (0)703 661 1581; fax: +1 (0)703 661 1547; email: styluspub@aol.com

For details of local agents and representatives in other countries, consult our website:
www.oxfam.org.uk/publications
or contact Oxfam Publishing, Oxfam House, John Smith Drive, Cowley, Oxford, OX4 2JY, UK
tel +44 (0) 1865 473727; fax (0) 1865 472393; email: publish@oxfam.org.uk

Our website contains a fully searchable database of all our titles, and facilities for secure on-line ordering.

Published by Oxfam GB, Oxfam House, John Smith Drive, Cowley, Oxford, OX4 2JY, UK

Printed by Information Press, Eynsham

Oxfam GB is a registered charity, no. 202 918, and is a member of Oxfam International.

Preface

In its analysis of the Kosovo crisis in 2001, ALNAP's first ever *Review of Humanitarian Action*, showed that humanitarian agencies did not give enough attention to people's protection. Many agencies focused on the provision of material assistance, leaving protection to mandated agencies such as UNHCR and ICRC. The *Review* concluded that the humanitarian community was at last waking up to the fact that all humanitarian agencies have a role to play in people's protection in war and disaster. Agencies realised that they have an obligation to work with communities, mandated agencies and responsible authorities to ensure people's safety as well as providing assistance to those in need.

But how? A search through ALNAP's database of evaluation reports revealed that there were alarmingly few evaluative reports that dealt with protection, in spite of its importance. Although some excellent publications were available elsewhere, there was little material available which was specifically tailored to help humanitarian practitioners think through the key issues and practicalities of protective programming. ALNAP member agencies therefore asked for this gap to be filled in the form of a guidance booklet on protection for humanitarian agency field staff.

After extensive consultation with protection specialists and with many agency staff throughout the ALNAP network, the *ALNAP Guidance Booklet for Humanitarian Protection – Pilot Version* was published in 2003 and then tested in the field by practitioners throughout 2004. It has been ALNAP's most popular publication to date suggesting that the need for guidance on protection is as great as ever. ALNAP is grateful to all those agencies who participated in the pilots and the lessons learned have been incorporated into this new first edition.

This new road-tested guide is now better equipped to help practitioners get to grips with both the concepts that underpin protection and the operational elements involved. Sections 1-3 will help people understand the context of people's protection needs and also provides an important framework for understanding protection in terms of responsibility and action. Sections 4-8 offer a practical schema designed to help agency staff think through the practicalities of protection focused programming in four clear steps: assessment; programme design; implementation, monitoring and evaluation.

It is well understood that this guide is not a panacea and that people's protection in war and disaster will continue to be a very difficult undertaking. But all of us in ALNAP share the hope that this guide will have significant value in helping to ensure the safety and dignity of those people who need it most.

John Mitchell, Head of ALNAP

Acknowledgements

Many people have helped us to research and write this booklet. As co-author of the original pilot version, Luis Enrique Eguren has also had a significant influence on the approach and content of the final guide.

In early discussions and through their important writings on the subject, Diane Paul, James Darcy and Paul Bonard also helped to shape the project.

As members of the project's two advisory groups, Alain Aeschlimann, Asmita Naik, Geeta Narayan, Nadya Kebir Raoloson, Sarah Wikenczy, Anita Menghetti, Shahrzad Tadjbakhsh and Marc Vincent each gave us vital comments from their careful readings of early drafts.

Liam Mahoney and David Petrasek gave a particularly helpful steer on how humanitarian and human rights perspectives overlap.

Brian Phillips, Wayne McDonald, Ed Schenkenberg, Danielle Coquoz, Jenny McAvoy, Gina Pattugalan, Bjorn Pettersson, Simon Lawry-White, Gabriele Russo, Kate Mackintosh, Peter Giesen, Peter Klanso, Kamela Usami, Mark Vincent, Kathrin Starup, Nicoletta Pergolizzi, Ermino Sacco, Christophe Beau, Romain Sirois, Nicholas Crawford and Karin Landgren also contributed many important suggestions.

Finally, at ALNAP, John Mitchell managed and supported the whole project with a calm professionalism for which we are most grateful.

Hugo Slim and Andrew Bonwick

Acronyms and abbreviations

FAO	Food and Agriculture Organisation (UN)
HIV	human immunodeficiency virus
ICRC	International Committee of the Red Cross
IDP	internally displaced person
IHL	international humanitarian law
IHRL	international human rights law
ILO	International Labour Organisation (UN)
IOM	International Organisation for Migration (UN)
NGO	non-governmental organisation
OCHA	Office for the Coordination of Humanitarian Affairs (UN)
OHCHR	Office of the High Commissioner for Human Rights (UN)
PRA	participatory rural appraisal
SRSG	Special Representative of the Secretary-General
UNHCR	United Nations High Commissioner for Refugees (UN)
UNICEF	United Nations Children's Fund (UN)
WFP	World Food Programme (UN)
WHO	World Health Organisation (UN)

Table of contents

Checklists

Checklists are featured throughout the booklet, which are intended to act as a practical prompt for fieldworkers, and identify the key skills required for assessment and analysis of protection programming:

Boxes

introduction

How can people at risk in war and disaster be better protected? And what practical role can humanitarian agencies and their staff play in helping to bring about such protection on the ground? This guide aims to provide some answers to these questions, and is intended as a practical guide for field staff in humanitarian agencies.

Introduction

Many millions of civilians continue to be deliberately targeted in war today, or suffer from the extreme consequences of armed conflict with its inevitable disruption, deprivation, displacement, disease and discrimination. Millions of others need protection in the many natural disasters or protracted social conflicts that come to dominate their lives. People at risk are usually the main actors in their own protection – making extraordinary efforts to protect themselves and their families. But there is also much that humanitarian agencies can do to help them and to mobilise responsible authorities.

A concern for human rights, international humanitarian law and refugee law has been integrated into the policies and practice of internationally mandated humanitarian agencies and many non-governmental organisations (NGOs). But a new determination to develop truly practical programming that protects people from all forms of violation, exploitation and abuse during war and disaster has emerged in recent years. Fieldworkers in both types of humanitarian organisation are now expected to know about protection and be able to work as much for people's protection as for their physical needs. They are also expected to train others to do so too. This involves an active concern for people's personal dignity as well as for their safety and material needs.

Despite all this goodwill, ensuring people's protection is extremely difficult and is the legal responsibility of *de jure* or *de facto* authorities in a given situation. These authorities are usually governments, international peacekeeping forces or armed groups. Humanitarian agencies are rarely in a position to protect anyone directly from the violent assaults, terror tactics, displacement and dispossession that cause so much suffering and destitution to the victims of war and disaster. As a result, and particularly in war, humanitarian agency personnel have often felt like bystanders to atrocity. Much of the advice offered in this guide inevitably concentrates, therefore, on more indirect approaches to protection. Here, there are important things that humanitarian agencies can do in addition to and alongside their primary role of providing aid and assistance to those who suffer.

Most immediately of all, humanitarian agencies can work practically and carefully with affected populations to support concrete ways in which they can avoid and resist the threats ranged against them as they cope with constant danger. Humanitarian field staff can also use their presence on the ground creatively to witness violations and unacceptable conditions and to deter further abuses. Agencies can also work hard to ensure that the humanitarian assistance programmes they design and deliver do not thoughtlessly expose civilian populations to yet more dangers from raiding, exploitation, rape, isolation, permanent displacement or corruption, and so inadvertently supporting those pursuing war or personal enrichment.

Politically, humanitarian agencies can also work to influence the responsible authorities, and so play their part in important local, national and international efforts to ensure respect for the norms, rights and duties set out in international law. Holding the appropriate authorities responsible and accountable is critical in protection work. A great part of this involves putting pressure on and working with those with legal responsibility for protection – state authorities, international peacekeeping forces and *de facto* authorities like armed groups. Much of it also involves liaising closely with other international organisations with protection mandates, such as the International Committee of the Red Cross and United Nations agencies like the Office of the High Commissioner for Human Rights (OHCHR), the United Nations High Commission for Refugees (UNHCR) and the United Nations Office for the Coordination of Humanitarian Affairs (OCHA) and other specialist UN agencies, so that they too bring their influence to bear on those responsible.

Finally, humanitarian organisations can work long-term to influence the deeper values of violent, war-torn and disaster-prone societies so that the principles of human dignity and protection are more broadly embraced by the hearts, minds and institutions of a society.

Focus on safety, dignity and integrity of the individual

The approach used in this guide is intended to help every humanitarian agency to look beyond people's immediate material needs to wider questions of personal safety and the dignity of the whole human person. As such, it draws attention to the main violations and abuses that are most likely to threaten people's safety, dignity and integrity as human beings. It then challenges agencies to think creatively about a range of ways in which such violation and suffering can be prevented, alleviated and redressed beyond a simple 'aid-only' approach.

An emphasis on civilians

The guide maintains a predominant emphasis on civilian populations affected by war but applies equally to people's protection needs in natural disasters and protracted social conflicts involving consistent violations and abuses of human rights.

In concentrating on civilians in war, however, it is appreciated that civilians are not the only people in need of protection in war. Members of state armed forces or armed groups are also entitled to certain forms of protection, which are determined by rules guiding the conduct of hostilities. When wounded or captured, they are entitled to important protection guarantees. However, the particular needs of these important groups are not considered here.

The purpose of this guide

This guide aims to introduce and illustrate this approach to protection so that humanitarian agency staff members are in a better to position to judge whether and how to engage in protection work. The guide is broadly organized into two parts. Part One (sections 1–3) is a general introduction to the concept of protection. It looks at why people need it, who is responsible for it and how humanitarian agencies can best think about it in their work alone and in complementary partnerships with others. It also alerts agencies to certain key risks of protective programming. Part Two (4–8) builds on a risk-based model of protection to offer a four step operational framework for assessing, designing, implementing and monitoring humanitarian work with clear protection objectives.

In particular, the guide will:

- **describe the thinking and objectives behind protection work**

- **identify the key elements of basic programming that enable agencies to be more protection-focused in their work**

- **offer some general guidance on how to monitor protection work**

- **alert agencies to the risks of pursuing protection objectives.**

Above all, it is hoped that the following pages will help people in humanitarian agencies to be more conscious of the possible protection opportunities in their work, and so make more informed choices about what to do and when and how to do it.

The guide's methodology also aims to increase the level of results-based reporting on protection objectives in humanitarian programmes. Better objective-setting and monitoring will then serve to improve agency learning and practice. It will also enable future ALNAP *Reviews of Humanitarian Action* to draw wider conclusions about protection across the humanitarian sector as a whole.

General guidance only

This guide is not a comprehensive field manual. It does not go into great detail on specific methodologies essential to protection activities – like needs assessment, monitoring human rights and international humanitarian law (IHL), security analysis, capacity-building, advocacy or interagency cooperation. It does not examine the detailed rights, experiences and likely protection needs of particular groups of people in war, such as women, children, the elderly, minorities, the displaced and refugees.

Instead, it aims to point field personnel from any humanitarian agency in the right direction when they are considering or managing any form of humanitarian action that seeks to protect people from the violations, abuses and consequences of war. It assumes that all agencies are well aware of the operational demands of their particular mandate and the mandates of other relevant organisations. It also takes for granted that each agency has considerable understanding of the experience and needs of the particular groups it is seeking to help, and significant expertise in the sectors in which its works.

The guide needs to be used alongside:

- **international legal standards in humanitarian, human-rights and refugee law**

- **detailed best-practice guides for protecting particular groups**

- **good-practice guidance for technical assistance programming in specific sectors like water, food and health – much of which can be found in the Sphere standards.**

How the guide was written

This guidance booklet draws on many of the excellent and important new policy papers, agency guidelines and manuals that have been written on this topic in recent years, including those which emerged from the pioneering series of workshops on Protection for Human Rights and Humanitarian Organisations convened annually by ICRC in Geneva from 1996–2000. Many of these are listed below in Annex 1. This guide attempts to place key principles and ideas from these works in one place, so that humanitarian agencies have a general field guide for designing and managing protective programming.

Several of the examples of protective humanitarian programming in this guide are taken from the 2002 IASC publication on protection, *Growing the Sheltering Tree: Protecting Rights through Humanitarian Action*, which is a rich source of practical examples of recent agency protection activities.

Structure of the guide

This guide is organised into nine main sections.

Part 1: Understanding protection

Section 1 identifies the different contexts in which protection is a priority for humanitarian agencies, and looks at the main forms of deliberate personal violence, deprivation and restricted access that create protection needs.

Section 2 uses the principle of humanity to define protection in terms of a person's safety, dignity and integrity as a human being. It then looks at the main sources of protection in international law, the primacy of state responsibility for protection, and agencies with protection mandates.

Section 3 introduces the egg framework for protection, its three spheres of action and its emphasis on complementarity within the international system for protection. It also identifies a number of common operational risks in protection work.

Part 2: Programming for protection

Section 4 introduces a risk-based model for protection work that concentrates on reducing threats, vulnerability and danger time.

Section 5 offers a particular approach to situation analysis and gives guidance on making a protection assessment using a range of checklists and information-gathering techniques.

Section 6 introduces the idea of protection outcomes and objectives as the key planning instrument from which to design and monitor a protection programme.

Section 7 examines five main modes of protection action appropriate to humanitarian agencies, with checklists on good practice. It also includes a case-study example of designing protection objectives in a humanitarian programme.

Section 8 gives general guidance on how to use protection outcomes and protection indicators to monitor the success or failure of protection work.

Section 9 finishes the guide with a summary of eight best-practice principles for effective protection work by humanitarian organisations.

Following these nine main sections, the **Bibliography** provides a list of full reference details, further reading and resources for protective programming, **Annex 1** lists the most relevant international and regional legal standards for humanitarian protection, and **Annex 2** summarises the UN's checklist of key actions for the protection of civilians.

1

part one
understanding protection

1 | 1

section **one**

Protection from what?

Perhaps the easiest way to understand the practicalities of protection is to think about the people who need it most, their experience in war and disaster, and the violations and abuses that they face.

In April 1991, in the midst of the first coalition war against Iraq, a picture of a little girl in the holy city of Safwan made a big impression on humanitarian agencies and political commentators. In a crowd of IDPs, this destitute but dignified child stood with a placard around her neck. On it was an inscription that read: 'We don't need food. We need safety'.[1] That food and safety, dignity and protection are integrally related as vital components of humanitarian action is an obvious truth. But it is one that is deeply difficult to realise when warring parties are intent on involving civilians or unable to protect them. Or when certain communities are marginalised or discriminated against in disasters.

If the little girl in Safwan needed personal protection rather than food, many other people affected by war or disaster are frequently in desperate need of both and all the other crucial elements of assistance, such as healthcare, shelter, water and sanitation. Beyond their immediate right to life, the reality of war, disaster and protracted social conflict for many people is just one massive violation of the whole range of their civil, political, economic, social and cultural rights.

Variety of contexts

Protection needs arise in a variety of situations in which humanitarian agencies tend to be involved, but particularly perhaps in five main situations, as follows.

1   **Armed conflict** – either international or non-international armed conflict in which the civilian population suffers a range of deliberate violations and abuses as well as the terrible but unintended consequences of war.

2   **Post-conflict situations** – in which a peace has been agreed but the effective rule of law is not yet complete, so that violations and abuses persist and conditions frequently remain life-threatening and personally degrading.

[1] Roberts, A (1996) *Humanitarian Action in War: Aid, Protection and Impartiality in a Policy Vacuum*. Adelphi Paper 305. Oxford: Oxford University Press for the International Institute for Strategic Studies (IISS), p 39.

3   **Natural disasters** – in which a natural hazard combines with poverty and social vulnerability to render people materially, personally and socially at extreme risk.

4   **Famine** – where drought, discrimination, political mismanagement and/or deliberate starvation cause severe food shortages, destitution and severe economic, social and personal risk.

5   **Protracted social conflict** – civil strife or political oppression that falls short of official armed conflict but nevertheless involves a crisis in which discrimination, violence, exploitation and impoverishment are constant risks.

In all five of these main contexts of humanitarian action, people are exposed to extreme levels of risk and can be forced to engage in equally perilous and exploitative coping or survival strategies. As a result, agencies operating in any one of these contexts are likely to encounter a broad and sometimes similar range of protection needs arising from various violations and deprivations, examples of which are given in Box 1 (overleaf). These various forms of suffering and indignity are typically the result of the triple dangers of deliberate personal violence, deprivation and restricted access. These pose extreme risks that continue to prove calamitous or fatal to many millions of people in war and disaster.

Box 1

Violations and deprivations that cause protection needs

- Deliberate killing, wounding, displacement, destitution and disappearance.
- Sexual violence and rape.
- Torture and inhuman or degrading treatment.
- Dispossession of assets by theft and destruction.
- The misappropriation of land and violations of land rights.
- Deliberate discrimination and deprivation in health, food, education, property rights, access to water and economic opportunity.
- Violence and exploitation within the affected community.
- Forced recruitment of children, prostitution, sexual exploitation and trafficking (including by peacekeepers and humanitarian staff), abduction and slavery.
- Forced or accidental family separation.
- Arbitrary restrictions on movement, including forced return, punitive curfews or roadblocks which prevent access to fields, markets, jobs, family, friends and social services.
- Thirst, hunger, disease and reproductive health crises caused by the deliberate destruction of services or the denial of livelihoods.
- Restrictions on political participation, freedom of association and religious freedom.
- The loss or theft of personal documentation that gives proof of identity, ownership and citizen's rights. Attacks against civilians and the spreading of landmines.

Deliberate personal violence

Direct personal violence in armed conflict, post-conflict or protracted social conflict is a common cause of suffering and death. The deliberate murder of civilians – women, men and children – has been central to the policies of belligerents in most recent wars.

The vicious use of sexual violence against civilians has also been central to the policies and practices of many of those pursuing war. Beyond the immediate humiliation, outrage and social impact of sexual violence, the spread of the human immunodeficiency virus (HIV) is an increasing and frequently deliberate result of such strategies of personal violence.

Children have been murdered routinely in recent wars just as they have been throughout history. They have also been brutally coerced into becoming child soldiers and prostitutes or forced into circumstances so terrible that taking on such roles emerges as the best choice open to them.

In addition to killings and sexual violence, hundreds of thousands of people have experienced the most vicious personal injuries. Some of these have come from the fierce blow of a machete or the force of a rifle butt. Others have been maimed forever by deliberate signature atrocities such as amputation in Sierra Leone, or having their lips and ears cut off in northern Uganda. Others have been wounded for life by the ongoing and indiscriminate injuries caused by landmines. Millions of women, men and children have been left emotionally wounded and economically and socially vulnerable as widows, widowers or orphans.

The extent of these atrocities means that humanitarian action focused primarily on assistance can fall well short of protecting people's dignity and integrity or meeting their urgent need for safety. People obviously require personal protection as well as food aid and healthcare if they are not to become the 'well-fed dead' who were so lamented during the war in Bosnia.

Deprivation

Despite the scale of such direct personal atrocity, it is impoverishment, dispossession, destitution, disease and sheer exhaustion that are responsible for the bulk of civilian deaths in war. Throughout the 1990s, most civilians died *from war* rather than violently *in war*. This is true of most wars that do not involve the mass slaughter of civilians.

The deprivations caused by war – what people have taken away from them – often become the determinant factor in people's suffering. Deliberate assaults on economic assets and livelihoods plunge people into poverty and threaten them with destitution and disease. Deliberate strategies of displacement and punishment mean that villages are burned, wells are poisoned, cities ransacked and homes bulldozed. Policies of terror, dispersal and restricted movement have ensured that people have lost access to their fields, natural resources, jobs and markets. Small businesses are attacked, cattle raided and people made to become forced labourers for those using war to secure the riches offered by the exploitation of diamonds, drugs, oil and timber. The destruction of social and cultural assets like schools, clinics, churches, mosques, temples and cemeteries, or a loss of access to them, have an extreme physical, social and emotional impact. Possessions are also routinely stolen in the endless pillaging that is a feature of so many wars.

These deprivations are all deliberate violations and abuses of a person's right to property, livelihood, education and health, as well as to free association, freedom of religion and cultural autonomy. Ultimately, they can prove socially devastating and individually fatal, which is frequently the intention.

Limited movement and restricted access

In war and after some natural disasters, authorities often deliberately restrict people's movements by imposing curfews, enforcing roadblocks and travel restrictions closing borders or forcibly returning people to unsafe areas. Warring parties can often deliberately destroy economic, health and educational facilities like schools, markets and clinics. Such restriction and destruction can make access to important places and facilities impossible for people. Often, these strategies of restriction and destruction go well beyond legitimate military necessity and are part of a wider policy of oppression, punishment, marginalisation and group-targeted violence.

Even when local services are not directly destroyed or depleted and when no explicit restrictions are in force, people may still be too afraid to move and access the places and facilities they need. The intense fear resulting from surrounding patterns of violence can intimidate people sufficiently to make them restrict or alter their own movement dramatically, putting great pressure on their ability to survive.

Fear of violence can stop people working their fields, going to markets or using certain roads. It can make them give up using essential social services like schools and clinics. It can prevent them from taking up the assistance offered by humanitarian agencies if the journey to acquire it is considered to be too dangerous. In cities, fear can force people into siege conditions. Maintaining or recovering people's access to key social and economic services is one of the biggest challenges in protection work.

In many cases, force and fear may impel people not to restrict their movement but to extend it dramatically by becoming refugees or internally displaced persons (IDPs). Extreme movement of this kind creates similar problems of access, as people are usually forced to flee to areas where services are limited, congested or non-existent. In such situations, ensuring safe access to basic services becomes a major protection challenge.

In many situations, protection challenges are problems of safe access. People's fear or inability to gain access to their means of livelihood, healthcare and social care results in significant suffering. The frequent inability of humanitarian agencies to reach threatened populations because of political or military restriction increases this further.

The question of intent

The political, military and individual intent behind particular violations and abuses in war and disaster is a critical issue in protection work. Whether or not suffering is intentional determines the nature of the protection challenge your agency confronts. An enormous amount of civilian suffering in war is intentional. It is the result of deliberate and preconceived strategies of violence, discrimination, displacement and deprivation. This can also be the case in famine, post-conflict, protracted social conflict and with the policies directed at disaster-affected populations.

When suffering is intentional, people's protection is hard-won and the protection challenge faced by a humanitarian agency is usually enormous. If people want to kill, violate, displace, marginalise and impoverish, then humanitarian workers are not particularly well placed to stop them. In such situations, an agency's protection activities will be working *against* the intentions of the legal or *de facto* authorities and armed groups perpetrating these abuses. Humanitarian personnel will be seen more as a threat than an ally by such negative authorities. Inevitably, room for manoeuvre will be restricted and the strategies and modes of action you choose will be politically complicated. These situations are more likely to raise difficult programming choices between access, compromise and confrontation.

In other cases, suffering is not intentional and you can find yourself working with essentially cooperative and positive authorities. In some wars, civilian suffering may be an unintended consequence that is genuinely regretted by one or more of the belligerents, who may then seek to protect and assist the civilians. In other situations, authorities may simply be overwhelmed by war. They may want to stop civilian suffering but be in no position to do so. In either context, your agency may be able to engage in cooperative protective activities with state or non-state parties, essentially working *with* the authorities concerned rather than against them. This will have many advantages. While there may still be enormous protection challenges, you may be better able to operate in modes that are collaborative and more akin to a partnership.

In many situations, humanitarian agencies face a spectrum of intent within a given authority. For example, some parts of the state authorities will be deliberately perpetrating violations while others will be genuinely trying to mitigate extreme state policies and improve people's conditions. The same range of abusive and protective intent can exist within an armed group. Understanding the range of intentions within a given authority becomes a critical part of protection analysis and response.

1 | 2

section **two**

Protection and responsibility

This section describes the basic concept of protection, the laws that demand it, the authorities that are required to provide it, and how the international system is intended to work to oversee and support people's protection.

Defining protection

Humanitarian agencies are moved to carry out humanitarian action by their most fundamental guiding principle – the principle of humanity. In his classic formulation of this principle the Swiss humanitarian, Jean Pictet, captures the essence of humanitarian action as being 'to protect life and health and to ensure respect for the human being'.[2]

The emphasis in this principle on the whole human being is critical. It recognises that we are more than flesh and blood. When we are cut we bleed and when we cannot drink we thirst; but beyond our material needs, we also feel and care – about ourselves and others. This sense of self-worth, and the deep value of being together in family and community of some kind, are as important to protect and assist as are our physical needs. We live emotionally, socially and spiritually as well as physically, and so we suffer emotionally, socially and spiritually too.

This most basic insight of humanitarian action makes clear that preserving a person's dignity and integrity as a human being is as much a goal in humanitarian work as ensuring their physical safety and providing for their material needs. The principle of humanity recognises human beings as much more than physical organisms in need of the means of survival. As such, humanitarian work extends beyond physical assistance to the protection of a human being in their fullness. This means a concern for a person's safety, dignity and integrity as a human being.

Safety

Effective protection helps people to stay safe. Good humanitarian work is as much about securing personal safety as it is about giving humanitarian assistance. Many agencies – mandated and non-mandated – have known the truth regarding this deeper definition of humanitarian action for many years. This is why they have dug wells and lobbied governments at the same time, provided food aid and educated soldiers on humanitarian law, vaccinated children and reported abuses that they have suffered.

[2] Pictet, Jean (1979) *The Fundamental Principles of the Red Cross: a Commentary.* Geneva: Henry Dunant Institute, p 18. The principle of humanity is also reaffirmed by the United Nations in General Assembly Resolution 46/182 of 1991.

Defining protection by safety outcomes – keeping people safe – gives a clear cutting edge to all humanitarian activities whether they are assistance, advocacy, community mobilisation or rights education. Personal safety is essential and must be at the forefront of all protection work. Prioritising personal safety in violent conflict and disaster gives very clear protection goals in any humanitarian programming and allows us to measure progress against them.

Dignity

But, of course, safety is not enough in itself. People might be extremely safe from military attack by staying in a heavily guarded 'protected village' or confined to their house under sustained curfew. They might be safe but may also be hungry, ill, isolated, increasingly impoverished and, above all perhaps, humiliated by the way they are treated by those guarding them.

Safety is fundamental to survival but the emotional and material quality of that safety is critical. The inner emotional experience of an individual is as important as their outward physical needs. And, of course, the two are intimately related. Terrible physical conditions can take a great toll on a person's dignity and sense of self-esteem. Yet, a person's ability to maintain a strong sense of personal identity and self-respect can hold them through extreme physical suffering.

Protection, therefore, is as much about preserving the dignity of the human person as it is about the safety of that person. Many violations, deprivations and restrictions degrade a person and are often designed to do so. They make people feel less than human by shaming them, tormenting them, disregarding them, dispossessing them or reducing them to conditions of hunger, nakedness and destitution which render them desperate and at odds with their neighbour and their family over the very means of survival.

Also essential to a sense of human dignity is the feeling of freedom. People who are free to live their lives as they choose, to move freely, to speak freely and to assemble and associate freely with others are more likely to experience that sense of self-worth and personal autonomy which is so important to human dignity.

All kinds of violations and abuses are attacks on the dignity of a person. To keep one's dignity is often the highest priority for people enduring war and disaster. If people lose a sense of themselves as free and valuable human beings, they are close to losing everything.

Integrity

The idea of integrity brings together the priorities of safety, dignity and material needs. It captures the importance of a person's completeness as a human being as a combination of physical, emotional, social, cultural and spiritual attributes.

The notion of integrity affirms that people need protecting in their wholeness. A person is entitled to enjoy life in its fullness, and is most human when they do so. To violate or deprive someone in any way is to attack and damage their integrity: it is to wound them physically, psychologically, emotionally or socially.

Protection as empowerment

Protection is fundamentally about people. It is a mistake to think of states, authorities and agencies as the sole actors in the protection of populations at risk. People are always key actors in their own protection.

Protection is not just a commodity or service that can be delivered like food or healthcare. It is also something that people struggle for and achieve within a given situation, or secure more widely in the politics of their own society. One of the most important aspects of protection is, therefore, people's ability to organise and claim it for themselves. Experience from many armed conflicts and disasters throughout history shows that human rights and humanitarian norms are most readily respected, protected and fulfilled when people are powerful enough to assert and claim their rights. The principle of supporting and empowering communities at risk that are actively working for their own protection – both practically and politically – needs to be maintained as a core strategy in protection work. Protection that is achieved by people, rather than delivered to them, is likely to be more durable.

Discussion of protection can often be heavily centred on institutions. But it is essential to ensure that protection is not merely a legal and programming conversation between agencies, states and armed groups that takes place over the heads of protected persons. On the contrary, wherever access and contact permit, protection work is also about working directly with people to support, identify and develop ways in which they can protect themselves and realise their rights to safety, assistance, repair, recovery and redress.

Protection as rights-based

This understanding of protection, with its emphasis on safety, personal dignity, integrity and empowerment, is understood by the great majority of governments and international agencies in terms of rights. It is internationally recognised that people have rights to protection, while authorities and individuals have legal obligations to respect the law and ensure protection.

This rights-based approach to protection is most clearly summarised by the consensus reached in 1999 by a wide group of humanitarian and human-rights agencies regularly convened by the ICRC in Geneva. This group affirmed that protection is:

> **'all activities aimed at ensuring full respect for the rights of the individual in accordance with the letter and the spirit of the relevant bodies of law, i.e. human rights law, international humanitarian law and refugee law. Human rights and humanitarian organisations must conduct these activities in an impartial manner and not on the basis of race, national or ethnic origin, language or gender'.**[3]

This rights and obligations approach to protection is rooted in the binding treaties and conventions of international law.

[3] Giossi Caverzasio, Sylvie (2001) *Strengthening Protection in War: a Search for Professional Standards.* Geneva: ICRC, p 19.

Law and protection

The Geneva Conventions and Additional Protocols – a key part of the international laws of armed conflict, commonly known as international humanitarian law (IHL) – identify civilians as an essential social group to be protected in armed conflict, because they do not take an active part in hostilities.

Refugee law makes it clear that refugees – as a particular group of civilians – who require asylum in another country are to be protected by the international community when their own state has failed to do so. The UN's 1998 Guiding Principles on Internal Displacement recognise that internally displaced persons (IDPs) – another large category of civilians – are equally protected by international human-rights law and international humanitarian law.

Alongside international humanitarian law and refugee law which specifically protect civilians in war, International Human Rights Law (IHRL) recognises that all people have certain fundamental and 'non-derogable' rights that must be protected at all times – even in conditions of war, disaster and emergency. These include:

- **the right to life**

- **the right to legal personality and due process of law**

- **the prohibition of torture, slavery and degrading or inhuman treatment or punishment**

- **the right to freedom of religion, thought and conscience.**

Various human-rights conventions outline many other more detailed civil, political, social, economic and cultural rights, including the rights of those most vulnerable to the abuse of power, including women, children and minorities.

The most serious violations of these various bodies of law may amount to *international crimes*, making their perpetrators liable to prosecution in international courts, and requiring all states to take appropriate action to ensure their punishment. In the past ten years, the international community has taken important steps to punish war crimes, crimes against humanity and genocide. The legal regimes constructed as a result are an important component of efforts to protect civilians in armed conflict.

In recent years, these bodies of law have been reaffirmed as the legal benchmarks of protection by several important resolutions of the United Nations Security Council. In particular, the Security Council is now committed to consider and prioritise the protection of civilians in armed conflict in all its decision making and in the relevant actions of UN member states.

Written into all these instruments of human rights, humanitarian and refugee law is the principle of respect for the safety, dignity and integrity of the human person. All these laws seek to ensure that in all situations people are to be treated humanely, that they should not be violated, abused, arbitrarily deprived or restricted and humiliated but be able to enjoy human life in its fullness. In practice, this means assuring a quality of individual life that is free from personal assault, sexual violation, degrading treatment and physical deprivation, and that is given sufficient civil, political, social, cultural and economic opportunity and autonomy.

Protection responsibility and protection mandates

Who has responsibility for ensuring that atrocity and deprivation do not happen in war? In other words, who is responsible for protection? Overall legal responsibility for protection lies with states as the signatories to the various instruments of international humanitarian law, human-rights law and refugee law. So, for example, international humanitarian law makes clear that states party to the Geneva Conventions 'undertake to respect and ensure respect for the Conventions in all circumstances'.[4]

State responsibility

States are the primary actors responsible for the protection of civilians in war. They are required to educate and control the conduct of all armed forces on their territory and to prosecute all those who breach international humanitarian law. When and where the protection of people has failed, and they become the victims of atrocity or deprivation, states are also required to meet their obligations to provide assistance for protected persons. At an individual level, commanders and members of armed forces and armed groups also have personal responsibility for violations of the law.

Where states cannot meet all of their humanitarian responsibilities directly, they are charged with enabling the provision of humanitarian action by impartial organisations. These organisations, in turn, are responsible for maintaining their impartiality – that is, by distributing aid on the basis of need alone. They are equally responsible for alerting the relevant authorities to protection failures and urging appropriate action. These *de jure* or *de facto* authorities may be governments, armed groups or peacekeeping forces.

This key principle that responsibility for protection in war and disaster lies primarily with state authorities and individual belligerents on all sides is affirmed in the 2004 guidance note issued to all United Nations Resident Coordinators and Humanitarian Coordinators:

[4] Geneva Conventions, Common Article 1.

Primary responsibility for ensuring the protection of people affected by conflict rests with the national authorities, as prescribed by international human rights law. Additional legal responsibilities can be imposed under international humanitarian law on combatants in armed conflict (including non-state armed groups) and on occupying powers. Some agencies/offices, such as ICRC, UNHCR, UNICEF and OHCHR, are mandated with protection responsibilities for specific categories or groups of persons. These are considered 'protection mandates'.[5]

This legal understanding of people's protection in war is fundamental to protection work. The law provides important international standards for how people can legitimately expect to be treated. The law can also form a powerful part of any argument to persuade individuals and governments to take certain actions in a given situation. As importantly, the law is also the essential instrument in efforts to hold states and individuals accountable for their actions and inactions towards civilians in war.

Mandated and specialised agencies

Several internationally mandated humanitarian and human-rights organisations are charged by states to lead on particular aspects of humanitarian protection and specific groups of protected persons. Among humanitarian agencies, the United Nations High Commissioner for Refugees (UNHCR) is internationally mandated to work with states to ensure the protection of refugees. The International Committee of the Red Cross (ICRC) has a particular mandate for overseeing the implementation and development of international humanitarian law and actively working with all parties in a conflict to protect persons affected by armed conflict, including civilians, detainees, prisoners of war and the wounded. The ICRC mandate also covers protection activities in situations of internal strife and in any situation requiring the involvement of a specifically neutral and independent institution or intermediary.

The mandates and roles of other important specialised agencies of the United Nations are also especially relevant in situations of war and disaster. The Office of the High Commissioner for Human Rights (OHCHR) has an international mandate to promote and protect human rights, to take action to

[5] UN IDP Division (2004) *Implementing the Collaborative Response to Situations of Internal Displacement, Guidance for UN Humanitarian and/or Resident Coordinators and Country Teams.* Geneva: UN IDP Division.

prevent human-rights violations and to work with states to realise all aspects of human rights. The Office for the Coordination of Humanitarian Assistance (UNOCHA) coordinates international humanitarian action and also supports the United Nations Security Council with its work on the protection of civilians. The United Nations Children's Fund (UNICEF) has a particular mandate to work with states to protect women and children. The UN Food and Agriculture Organisation (FAO) and the World Food Programme (WFP) are mandated to help states to meet their food-security responsibilities. The World Health Organisation (WHO) and the International Labour Organisation (ILO) are mandated to support state and international efforts to secure health and employment in line with international standards. The International Organisation for Migration (IOM) assists with the movement or voluntary return of endangered populations and is engaged in important counter-trafficking research and operations.

Non-mandated agencies

Other impartial humanitarian non-governmental organisations (NGOs) are also entitled to offer humanitarian action in support of persons affected by armed conflict and disaster. They make this offer on the basis of a particular humanitarian expertise, in accordance with national legislation in the country concerned and in line with the general principle that individuals and groups, as well as states, have a responsibility to promote and respect human rights.

The challenge of protection

The law, the legal principle of primary state responsibility and the mandates of particular human-rights and humanitarian agencies offer civilians important legal protection in war and disaster. However, people are not actually protected just because the law says that they are and because it identifies authorities with a duty to protect them. In many wars and disasters, laws are frequently broken consciously and purposively by all sides. In others, these laws are simply unknown and it remains an open question whether knowledge of them would affect the behaviour of the parties concerned. Often laws are broken and rights are violated most by those state authorities with the greatest responsibility for keeping them. In other situations, states that are willing to abide by these laws lack the power or means to do so.

The fact that international humanitarian law, human-rights law and refugee law are routinely and dramatically flouted creates the enormous protection needs that exist in so many armed conflicts and disasters. Despite laws and rights, people do not enjoy the protection to which they are entitled. Local, national and international enforcement mechanisms are not sufficient to apply the law in many places affected by war and disaster. The horrors of this implementation gap are painful features of many people's lives, and the determining factors in so many people's deaths.

The real challenges of protection work, therefore, are about not the sufficiency of law but the enforcement of law. The main protection challenges are highly practical ones of ensuring responsibility and enforcing good conduct on the ground so that people can live in safety and dignity.

In practice, this is a twofold challenge for humanitarian agencies – both strategic and tactical. The first challenge is a strategic political task to get responsible authorities to ensure respect for human rights and humanitarian norms across a given context. Much of this involves both urgent and long-term advocacy as well as structural support for national authorities and civil society movements to bring about a positive protection environment in society as a whole. The second challenge is a more immediate tactical task which requires humanitarian workers to work effectively with people at risk to create imaginative and effective ways of ensuring that their humanitarian programmes also meet people's practical protection needs amidst continuing violations and abuses on the ground.

1 | 3

section **three**

A framework
for protection

This section introduces the egg model of humanitarian action as a general framework in which to consider any protection action. It also emphasises the importance of complementarity within the international protection system. Finally, it identifies a number of core risks or operational dilemmas commonly encountered by humanitarian agencies trying to meet protection needs.

The egg framework

One widely recognised model of protection among humanitarian agencies is the so-called *egg model* which emerged from the interagency discussions on protection lead by ICRC.[6] This model uses the shape of an egg to think strategically about the different spheres of action in which protection needs to be addressed and the different types of activities required to meet protection needs.

Spheres of action

Three main spheres of protective action gravitate outwards from the point of violation.

1   The most immediate sphere of action is closest to the victims and the pattern of abuse to which they are subjected. This sphere demands a range of **responsive action** that aims to stop, prevent or alleviate the worst effects of the abuses.

2   Moving further outwards, the second sphere is more restorative and is concerned to assist and support people after violations while they live with the subsequent effects of a particular pattern of abuse. This sphere of action involves a range of **remedial action** to help people recover.

3   The third sphere of action is further away still from the point of violation and is concerned with moving society as a whole towards protection norms which will prevent or limit current and future violations and abuses. This is the most long-term and structural sphere of action and requires **environment-building action** that consolidates political, social, cultural and institutional norms conducive to protection.

[6] Giossi Caverzasio, Sylvie (2001) *Strengthening Protection in War: a Search for Professional Standards.* Geneva: ICRC.

Box 2

Types of protection activity

Environment-building action is aimed at creating and/or consolidating an environment — political, social, cultural, institutional, economic and legal — conducive to full respect for the rights of the individual. Environment building is a deeper, more structural process that challenges society as a whole by aiming to change policy, attitude, belief and behaviour. It is likely to involve the establishment of more humane political values, improvements in law and legal practice, the training of security forces, and the development of an increasingly non-violent public culture.

Responsive action is any immediate activity undertaken in connection with an emerging or established pattern of violation and aimed at preventing its recurrence, putting a stop to it, and/or alleviating its immediate effects. Responsive activities have a sense of real urgency (but can last for many years) and aim to reach a particular group of civilians suffering the immediate horrors of a violation. They are primarily about stopping, preventing or mitigating a pattern of abuse.

Remedial action is aimed at restoring people's dignity and ensuring adequate living conditions subsequent to a pattern of violation, through rehabilitation, restitution, compensation and repair. Remedial activities are longer term and aim to assist people living with the effects of a particular pattern of abuse. This might include the recuperation of their health, tracing of their families, livelihood support, housing, education, judicial investigation and redress.

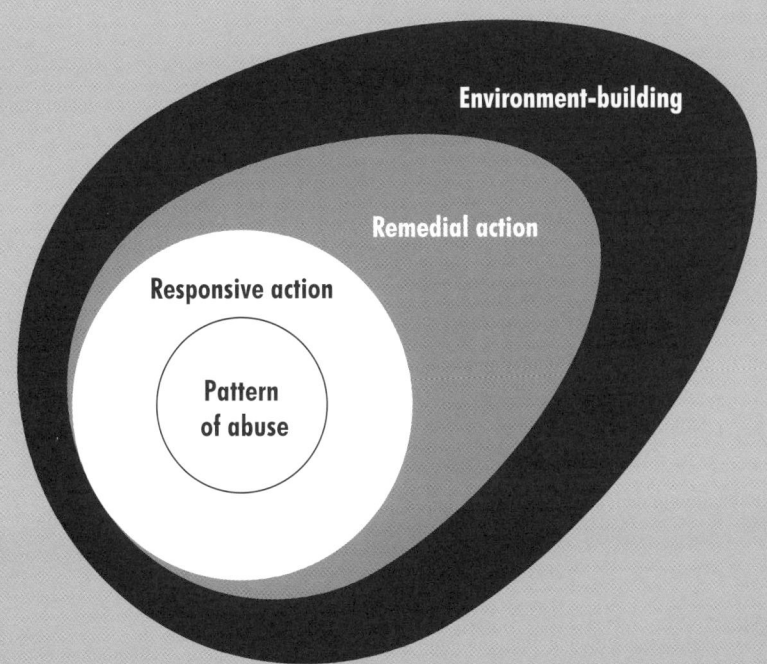

Source: Inter-Agency Standing Committee (2002) Growing the Sheltering Tree: Protecting Rights through Humanitarian Action, Programmes and Practices Gathered from the Field. Geneva: Inter-Agency Standing Committee, p 115.

Complementarity in protection work

As well as providing a useful framework for planning individual agency activities, the egg model with its three spheres of action provides a very useful way of looking at protection work at the system level by distinguishing between responsive, remedial and environment-building activities and considering which protection actor is best placed to pursue which action in a given situation. In other words, it allows humanitarian agencies to think together about how different agencies can complement one another in their efforts to work with authorities, with each other, with people at risk and with civil society movements to realise protection.

The key concept of complementarity emphasises the importance of diversity and cooperation in the protection system. Complementarity is perhaps best understood by analogy with a musical orchestra or band. All the instruments in the orchestra are important and each one needs to play its part if the orchestra is to interpret the music effectively. But every type of instrument plays different parts and not every kind of instrument is needed in every passage of the music. So, in some places the drums are essential and loud. In others they are silent. In some places the violins dominate, in others it is the woodwind or the brass. In vital moments, both loud and soft, all instruments boom or quietly tremble together. This is complementarity – each instrument playing according to the needs of the music.

Interagency complementarity for protection means that agencies will often be involved in different spheres of action and in different activities but the sum of their parts must all add up to better protection. The musical analogy begs the question of the conductor in protection work. The answer to this will differ depending on the situation. Sometimes the government itself will conduct. Sometimes people's movements from the population at risk will dominate the process and call the tune as they have tried to do in Colombia, for example. At other times, there will be a United Nations *maestro* in the form of a Special Representative of the Secretary-General (SRSG). And sometimes, complementarity will emerge from a genuine team effort among humanitarian agencies.

A concerted effort by all agencies to use their different mandates, expertise, resources and networks to meet commonly identified protection needs and desired outcomes for threatened populations can dramatically increase the likelihood of that protection being realised. Complementarity does not mean every agency doing the same thing. Instead, it involves each agency doing what it does best and what it is best placed to do. Such diversity of programming but unity of effort can be a significant protection multiplier.

Checklist A

Interagency complementarity

To achieve effective complementarity in and around your programme, a careful assessment must be carried out of the different mandates, strategies, capabilities and intentions of the many international agencies, government departments, NGOs and people's organisations operating in the situation. From this, a joint strategy that identifies different activities and plays to the comparative advantage of different agencies can be agreed and pursued. See also Section 7 on using the complementarity matrix.

- Understand the different mandates, programming capacities, priorities, expertise and 'added value' of other agencies and organisations.

- Assess the best way to combine different agencies working in different modes so that they complement one another's efforts in the best interests of protected persons, and avoid contradicting or jeopardising one another's strategies and activities.

- Consider setting up an interagency 'focal point' for protection or a 'protection working group' with the power to convene meetings, share information and analysis, agree protection priorities, and coordinate complementary agency strategies.

- Include other key international parties with humanitarian responsibility in your assessment, such as peacekeeping forces and international negotiators.

- Appraise the levels of trust between agencies and the degree to which they share common protection objectives.

Key protection skills

- Interagency liaison
- cooperation, and
- coordination

Recognising protection dilemmas

The need to operate humanitarian programmes protectively in highly contested, dangerous and deeply politicised conditions often presents real operational dilemmas for humanitarian agencies. Securing people's protection when others are out to do them terrible harm or to discriminate against them is a highly complicated task. It can verge on the impossible and routinely involves a number of strategic risks for humanitarian organisations – obvious programming 'traps' which need to be anticipated and avoided wherever possible.

Eight strategic risks in protection work

1   The **increased risks to victims** that your fact-finding, activities and behaviour may present. Insensitive or unprofessional behaviour and advocacy by humanitarian staff can expose particular individuals and civilian communities to heightened risk by leading to punitive backlashes or accelerated military action by authorities and armed groups. More generally, aid assets and sanctuary can be co-opted and abused by belligerents. Corruption in aid distribution can also render civilian populations vulnerable to extortion, threat and deprivation.

2   The risk that **aid is incorporated into abusive strategies**. Humanitarian activities or resources can be exploited and anticipated by the perpetrators of human-rights violations to facilitate abuses like forced displacement or raiding.

3   The risk of inadvertently **legitimising violations or perpetrators**. Deliberate starvation, for example, can be legitimised simplistically as 'famine' by aid workers unable to see the political intent behind it. The contact between state or non-state perpetrators and humanitarian agencies and their permission for token operations can be used cynically by perpetrator groups to give them political credibility and as evidence of a false intention to protect.

4   The **possibility or perception of bias** in difficult aid-targeting decisions. Humanitarian organisations often face real difficulty in being completely impartial. Limited access or resources often forces agencies to give apparent priority to one group of victims over another. This can happen as much with protection programming as in assistance and be seen as taking sides.

5   An active concern for protection-focused work often risks **politicising humanitarian action in the eyes of belligerents** who see criticism of any kind as a violation of humanitarian impartiality and may act against humanitarian agencies accordingly.

6   The risk that **donor governments over-emphasise protection by humanitarian agencies** and invest in agency protection activities as a substitute for driving forward their own proper state-level political action to address and stop violations.

7   The risk that the **work of humanitarian agencies becomes skewed towards protection activities** and does not pay sufficient attention to feeding and sheltering people and providing them with clean water and health-care.

8   The constant struggle to decide wisely in **a hard choice between two mutually exclusive goods**. This most often arises when choosing between humanitarian access and advocacy, for example, when it is impossible for an agency to combine both.

Box 3

Summary of the principles of protection work

- Prioritise people's personal safety, dignity and integrity.

- Recognise people at risk as key actors in their own protection.

- Engage the legal responsibilities of authorities and individuals.

- Help key government and civil society actors to build a positive and long-term protection environment for all.

- Work in a complementary fashion on responsive, remedial and environment-building activities.

- Avoid increasing the risk to endangered populations by misconceived or badly implemented activities.

The safety of humanitarian personnel

Several of these risks illustrate the point that protection work – particularly in a hostile environment where the predominant political intent is to violate rather than to protect – can also be very dangerous for humanitarian agency staff. Many of the objectives and activities suggested in this guide entail risks for humanitarian workers themselves. Fine judgements are required between courage and recklessness, effective action and dangerous gesture.

The safety of victims

Finally, the further risks to victims from agency activity cannot be emphasised enough. It is essential to keep constant watch on how your presence, personal contacts and various activities might expose affected communities and particular individuals to even more risk. Sometimes, simply speaking to people may endanger them.

2 |

part two
programming for protection

2 | 4

section **four**

Humanitarian programming with protection objectives

This section introduces a distinct operational approach to protection that responds practically to people's protection needs by focusing on their vulnerability to particular violations and threats. It focuses on identifying specific and measurable protection outcomes which – if they are achieved – will make people physically safer, preserve their dignity and make them more economically and socially secure.

The approach draws on the risk model of natural disaster theory and encourages an outcome-based approach to protection work that concentrates on finding practical ways in which people will be better protected by themselves or by others.

A risk-based model of protection

The best way to think about protection is from the perspective of those who need it. This can be done by understanding people's protection needs in terms of threat, violation, vulnerability, capacity and risk. This approach uses a model of risk and response that is familiar to many humanitarian agencies from their work in natural disasters.[7]

This risk-based model means appreciating the precise nature of the threats and vulnerabilities people are experiencing and the capacities they have to prevent and cope with them. To help think this through, the following equation adapted from natural disaster theory provides a good starting point:

$$\textbf{Risk} \; = \; \textbf{(Threat + Vulnerability)} \times \textbf{Time}$$

You can use this equation to build up an analysis of people's protection needs in a given situation. In applying this equation, three main programming challenges emerge if you are to minimise the risk faced by communities: reducing threats, reducing vulnerability and reducing danger time.

Reducing threats: engaging responsibility

Reducing the level of threat is the first programming priority. This means trying to make states, armed groups and individuals meet their humanitarian responsibilities to protect people in war. This involves engaging those responsible – directly or indirectly – in an effort to prevent violations, end threats and respond to suffering.

[7] See, for example: Blaikie, P, et al (1994) *At Risk: Natural Hazards, People's Vulnerability and Disasters.* London: Routledge; Anderson, Mary and Peter Woodrow (1989) *Rising from the Ashes: Development Strategies in Times of Disaster.* Boulder, Colorado: Westview Press; Cuny, Fred (1999) *Famine, Conflict and Response: a Basic Guide.* West Hartford: Kumarian Press.

Box 4

The risk equation in practice

Women and girls collecting water from wells outside their small towns and villages run an increasing **risk** of rape as they face the **threat** of drunk conscript government soldiers manning checkpoints at the edges of the towns and of military incursions by sexually violent rebel forces also using the same water-points in no-man's land. The poor repair and dilapidation of municipal wells and pipework in the middle of their settlements is a key source of **vulnerability** for the community which gives women little choice but to spend more **time** each day making longer journeys into militarised territory.

Reducing vulnerability: involving communities

Protection policy can often sound very state-centric. But it is essential to recognise that humanitarian protection is not merely a legal and programming conversation between agencies, states and armed groups that takes place over the heads of the endangered population. On the contrary, wherever access and contact permits, humanitarian protection work is also about working directly with affected communities to identify and develop ways in which they can protect themselves and realise their rights to assistance, repair, recovery, safety and redress.

It is vitally important that people in need of protection are not seen just as the objects of state power but also as the subjects of their own protective capabilities. In many wars and disasters, people survive despite the state. In any protection programme, communities at risk must be recognised as protection actors as well as victims. States have obligations to protect people, but people's most critical protection strategies may often be their own.

Reducing danger time: limiting exposure

A sense of urgency and timing are crucial in any protection programme. Reducing the length of time for which people are exposed to risk, and mitigating the worst effects of particularly risky moments, are central to success. The longer people are exposed to certain threats the more they will suffer and die. This applies to situations of group risk like those endured by communities in the midst of hostile military action, and to more individual risk like that experienced by women collecting firewood or going to market.

Recognising primary and secondary risks

Humanitarian agencies often work with people after they have *already* been harmed, so helping them to survive and recover from violations and deprivations that have already occurred. But it is important to remember that actions which people take to secure their protection from old or *primary* risks may also expose them to new or *secondary* risks.

Well-developed protection programmes take account of both types of risk and aim for outcomes that address primary and secondary threats. For example, a programme may set out to reduce the primary threat of militia attacks in home areas so that people can return safely, *in parallel* with reducing the new secondary threat of sexual violence against women in displaced communities. An agency may provide livelihood opportunities with the aim of reducing the vulnerability of people to the primary threat of forced and unsafe return, *in parallel* with efforts to address the new secondary threat of abduction as people venture into riskier areas to trade their produce.

Programme design

Protection-focused programmes are no different from any other form of programme. They need to be planned and systematic, while also being open to important opportunities as they arise. While it is important to sit down and decide what to do as soon as possible, it is first important to introduce the idea of an overall protection strategy to drive your planning and activities.

Your overall protection programme should try to answer the following questions.

• **Who are you trying to protect?**

• **From what are you trying to protect them?**

• **What capacity do people have to protect themselves?**

• **How will you help them?**

• **What resources will you use?**

• **Who will you do it with?**

• **How will you know if you have succeeded?**

A good protection programme meets these challenges by coming up with:

• the best possible response to people's **immediate protection needs**

• the best possible **long-term reduction of threats and violations**

• the best possible **reduction of people's vulnerability** to those threats

• the best possible **development of people's own capacities**.

Your choice of strategy will determine where you place your operational emphasis and which modes of protective action you prioritise according to the outcomes that you want to achieve.

Four programming steps

Many different approaches to project planning are applicable in designing and implementing protection work. We have chosen to conceive of programming in terms of outcomes, objectives and activities. The following four sections of the guide now guide you through the four critical steps of the design and implementation of protection programmes.

• **Situation analysis, needs assessment and opportunities to intervene (Section 5).**

• **Agreeing outcomes and setting objectives (Section 6).**

• **Choosing protection activities (Section 7).**

• **Monitoring progress against protection outcomes (Section 8).**

In later sections, this guide describes how to programme this approach by using the project cycle common to all project management. Section 5 looks at needs and vulnerability assessment. Section 6 shows how to identify practical protection outcomes and define objectives. Section 7 then helps you to decide which activities to carry out to achieve results. Finally, Section 8 looks at how best to monitor a protection programme.

2 | 5

section **five**

Step one: situation analysis and protection assessment

This section of the guide now moves from a strategic discussion of protection theory to more practical advice on how to put such theory into practice. It offers guidance on the assessment and information-gathering phase of the project cycle.

1 | Situation analysis and protection assessment

2 | Setting protection outcomes and objectives

3 | Choosing protection activities

4 | Monitoring protection outcomes

Introduction

The first phase of any practical protection programme is one of analysis and assessment. This section aims to identify exactly which groups of people need protection from precisely what kind of threats, violations and effects of war and disaster. It also identifies appropriate opportunities for humanitarian agencies to intervene.

This involves a detailed examination of the nature of violations, threats and abuses and their impact on people's lives. It also involves an appraisal of the responsibility and capacity of states, non-state actors, humanitarian agencies, and understanding of the strategies that communities themselves are adopting to prevent, stop and ameliorate such actions and their consequences.

In doing so, it must be remembered that in the frequently fast-moving conditions of war and armed violence, your organisation's situation analysis and protection assessment need to be continuously updated in order to adjust your programme as events develop on the ground.

Awareness of all victim groups

The concern of an impartial humanitarian agency should extend to all people in need of protection. Every humanitarian agency needs to combine a *general awareness* of all protection needs in the immediate environment with a *particular focus* on the specific mandate group and agency expertise. This means that your protection programme should – to some degree – take account of all people if only to ensure that some authority or agency is responding actively to their protection needs. But, if you work for a specifically mandated or specialist agency, a particular group of people or a particular aspect of protection may be your primary concern.

The main areas that require significant assessment and analysis are:

- **understanding violations, threats and perpetrators**

- **monitoring human rights and international law**

- **assessing their impact and effect on people and communities**

- **mapping existing community protection strategies**

- **identifying relevant legal standards and responsibility**

- **mapping political commitment to protection.**

This section looks at each of these points in turn. It provides a brief checklist on each, which is intended to act as a practical prompt for fieldworkers, and also identifies the key skills required to carry out such assessment and analysis. Most of these skills should be well known to humanitarian agencies.

Information gathering

The process of collecting information as part of a protection assessment is often much more sensitive and delicate than in other areas of humanitarian work. Many of the techniques of information gathering may be the same but the highly political and dangerous environments in which you are using them makes information gathering highly risky for you and the people you are trying to help.

Information sources are likely to include key informants in government, armed groups, the media, academia, civil society, religious or humanitarian organisations. They will also include secondary sources such as published reports. But it is often the people at risk who know most about their predicament and have the greatest insight into the threats against them. In particular, they may have important information about:

• **the nature and timing of the threats and violations confronting them**

• **the identity, mindset and personalities of (and the relationships between) the people posing these threats**

• **the resources within their community**

• **the history of previous threats and coping mechanisms**

• **the practical possibilities and opportunities for resisting these threats**

• **the optimal linkage between their own response and that of an agency.**

It is vital to harness this knowledge, capacity and expertise and use it to maximum effect in your situation analysis, programme design and monitoring.

Methodologies to collect the information can vary widely from informal or semi-structured interviews, through focus-group discussions to the varied application of participatory rural appraisal (PRA) techniques or even a systematic survey.

Many of these activities will require discussion with the victims of violations. Whenever you or your staff are consulting with people, it is vital that you enable them to describe their experience of suffering and threat directly, that you record it accordingly, and that you cross-check it.

It is also essential that you respect the dignity and continuing safety of your informants and their confidentiality where necessary. Talking to you may sometimes put them at even greater risk and your enquiries may backfire terribly on them. In addition, discussing their suffering and loss may be a traumatic or a positive experience for people. Often it will be both. Sometimes it will raise expectations. Sometimes it will also be deeply frustrating, as they may already have shared their experience before with no obvious result.

Box 5

Examples of risk, threat, violation and perpetrators

Some 130,000 IDPs who have fled from a policy of murder, rape and displacement **perpetrated by** hostile militias are now facing the **risk** of forcible return by the national authorities who did nothing to prevent their forced displacement. Reluctant to return, they now face immediate new **threats** of physical force and intimidation by government **perpetrators**. In one camp, these threats have already begun to be realised in actual **violations** in the form of tear-gas attacks, the destruction of IDP shelters and forcing men, women and children onto trucks in an effort to empty the camps.

Violations, threats and perpetrators

The first critical step in a protection assessment is to gain sufficient understanding of the kinds of violations experienced by the civilian population, the continuing threats against them, and the nature, intent and organisation of the perpetrators.

Checklist B

Violations, threats and perpetrators

- Understand the precise nature, pattern and scope of the violations and threats faced by people in the areas you are concerned with. Assess, in particular, how they are arising either from acts of *commission* (things people are doing) or acts of *omission* (things people should be doing but are not) or both. Remember also that a fear of violence – whether well founded or not – can often have as great an impact on a community as violence itself.

- Understand who is most vulnerable to the threats. This may involve important differentiation of the threats by age, gender, ethnic group, social status, religion or other factors.

- Find out if there is a particular pattern, timing, schedule, logic or symbolism connected with the threats and so if they might be predictable in any way, and gauge whether there are any factors (physical, social, spatial, economic, political and habitual) that may render people more at risk.

- Clarify exactly who is responsible for previous violations and current threats, what authority they have and what resources they are using. Understand precisely how, when and where they are committing such abuses. Identify critical factors that facilitate violations, including the availability of small arms and light weapons. And identify those who are turning a 'blind eye' to the violations or initiating strategies of denial.

- Understand *why* they are pursuing a policy of violations. What prejudices, reasons, interests, frustrations and emotions drive these strategies and how best can they be understood and challenged? Learn who is orchestrating, encouraging, permitting and colluding in the perpetration of violations, as ideologues, strategists, active supporters or deliberate bystanders.

- Attempt, on the basis of the above, to anticipate or predict the perpetrators' next steps. Recognise that they are likely to adjust their strategies to deflect efforts to stop them.

Monitoring human rights and international humanitarian law

The practice of IHRL and IHL monitoring and reporting is particularly important in protection assessment and situation analysis. Knowing precisely what violations and abuses are taking place can play an important role in assessing the risks that people are facing so that you can programme and advocate against them more effectively.

Proper and systematic IHRL and IHL monitoring requires care, resources and expertise. Some agencies may regard this type of monitoring as inappropriate to their mandate, tactically unwise or impractical because of inadequate levels of staff expertise. If this is so for your agency, it remains essential that you consider ways of alerting and involving other mandated humanitarian or human-rights organisations that are better placed to do this.

Box 6

Key terminology in human-rights and IHL monitoring

Monitoring is a broad term describing the active collection, verification and immediate use of information to address human-rights problems. It includes gathering information about incidents, observing events, visiting sites and discussions with government authorities to obtain information and to pursue remedies and other immediate follow-up.

Fact-finding is a narrower term than monitoring, and involves a great deal of information gathering in order to establish and verify facts surrounding an alleged human-rights violation or abuse.

Violations include governmental and non-state actors' transgressions of the rights guaranteed by national, regional and international human rights and humanitarian law, and acts and omissions directly attributable to the state or actor concerned involving failure to implement legal obligations derived from human-rights standards.

Abuses is a broader term than violations which is sometimes used in human-rights monitoring to refer to violative conduct committed by non-state actors.

Source: Adapted from UNCHR (2001) *United Nations Training Manual on Human Rights Monitoring.* Geneva: UNHCHR at < http://www.ohchr.org/english/about/publications/training.htm >

This work requires good knowledge of international legal standards. Equally, it requires sensitivity and the ability to listen carefully to people's accounts of their own experiences and those of others – especially in a climate of fear and conditions of continuing violation and abuse. Such due care is at once legal and interpersonal.

Checklist C

Monitoring and reporting violations and abuses of IHRL and IHL

- Consider the safety of the people who provide information, respect their confidentiality and constantly assess whether your monitoring activities are likely to put people at more risk.

- Know the international standards that are relevant to the mandate of your agency and applicable to the situation you are monitoring.

- Link people's experiences of violations and abuses to specific legal standards.

- Use your information to encourage and engage the actions of the responsible authorities.

- Be objective and consistent in how you interview, research and report so that your material is coherent and professional.

- Be precise and accurate in your recording of events and testimony, always working with a clear sense of how the information that you collect will be used.

- Cross-check and verify your information through a variety of sources.

- Respect the feelings and rights of witnesses during and after an interview in order not to humiliate or endanger them further.

- Where appropriate, be visible and transparent so that the authorities and the population concerned can see and understand what you are doing and why.

- Share the information you collect with other mandated agencies and with the organisations and members of the affected population wherever this is appropriate and likely to increase levels of protection.

Impact of violations on affected populations

The next key aspect of an assessment is to gain a precise understanding of the impact and effect of violations and threats on individuals and communities. Here it is particularly important to appreciate the different effects of threats and violation by assessing the secondary impact of violence. For example, even where the number of direct victims of violence is relatively low, whole communities may no longer feel safe to move their produce to market, and the economic impact can be devastating.

Checklist D

Impact and effects of violations

- Understand the primary and secondary effects of violations and threats on the people suffering them in physical, social, gender, health, economic, political, and emotional terms.

- Understand how different groups of people remain physically, socially, politically, economically and emotionally vulnerable to recent violations or future threats. This might include paying particular attention to the experience and needs of women, children, young men, the elderly or members of particular ethnic groups.

- Identify the immediate and longer-term needs for protection and assistance resulting from the impact of existing violations and continuing threats and differentiate between them more precisely in terms of age, gender, class or other groupings.

Community protection strategies

It is particularly important to understand how people are already coping with and even preventing violations and threats against them. Supporting community strategies can be the best form of action by humanitarian agencies.

Community protection strategies

- Understand the coping mechanisms and self-protection capabilities of protected persons and how they might best be supported and developed.

- What are people doing to *avoid* the threats that they face? Look at how people are changing their behaviour to reduce their vulnerability to the threats. Are people fleeing and becoming displaced? Are they changing their regular movements (eg not travelling on certain roads) or their daily routine? Are they keeping their heads down, hiding their assets and trying to become increasingly invisible? Are they setting up community early-warning systems in case of attack? Are people changing their livelihoods (eg planting crops only in areas around the village, not planting at all, migrating for work or going into prostitution) in order to survive?

- What is the impact of these changes and how long can people sustain them? What new risks do these coping strategies present?

- To what extent are people being forced to reach an accommodation with the violations and threats ranged against them? This may include obeying new orders, paying 'taxes' as protection money or becoming directly co-opted into new violence by joining militias or 'marrying' soldiers in armed groups. In short, is their adaptation to the threat positive or negative?

- What are communities doing to *confront* the threats? How are they organising? Are they arming themselves, fighting back, or even forming their own militias? Are they pursuing non-violent resistance of some kind? Are they dispirited and disintegrating as a community? Is it possible to support a growing pro-protection political mobilisation of civil society that is standing up to and challenging these threats with alternative humanitarian and human-rights values?

Legal standards and responsibility analysis

Having established the nature of violations and threats occurring in the area and their impact on particular groups, it is now possible and important to relate the situation to exact standards in international law. Law carries political power of its own and can be used as political leverage to influence the actions of authorities and individuals. In particular, a good legal analysis can serve three purposes.

First the law provides a benchmark to judge whether particular actions are acceptable or not. It is not difficult to work out that arbitrarily attacking clearly unarmed civilians while they are farming their fields is wrong and is a violation. But much of IHL and IHRL is a matter of more intricate legal interpretation. For example, what is the legal status of civilian building contractors who are killed during an assault on an army base? When is it acceptable for an occupying power to arrest and detain civilians? What restrictions can legitimately be placed on people's movement in a time of civil war? International law provides clarity and guidance to answer these questions.

Second, the law can be used to identify specific individuals, authorities, and agencies that have particular responsibilities for preventing, stopping, remedying and redressing violations and abuses in war. It can also clearly point to actions that make a perpetrator liable to prosecution and trial.

Finally, the law provides a more 'formal' description of abuses and people's subsequent suffering that gives due legal precision to otherwise vague political and diplomatic discourse. Such legal description is vital as a complement to more general and understandably emotive terms like attacks, violence, chaos, atrocities, suffering, and innocent people. It makes for more powerful rule-based arguments that can be used to persuade those responsible to take action.

Checklist F

Legal standards and responsibility analysis

- Determine which specific standards of national, regional and international law are relevant to the pattern of violations and threat in order to identify the laws, conventions, declarations and specific articles that clearly define what protection is afforded to whom in a given situation. Single out articles that refer expressly to the kinds of incidents observed and the strategies and policies functioning in this instance.

- Also take account of applicable domestic law that is not in contradiction with international standards (such as indigenous custom or shariah law) that may carry much weight locally and provide important protection guarantees.

- Clarify which authorities have primary responsibility for stopping the perpetrators under national and international law, and which other states have particular responsibility for responding to and halting these violations under international law.

- Clarify which authorities have responsibility for dealing with the *consequences* of the violations – for example providing for the basic needs of people forced from their homes or compensation for people whose assets have been destroyed.

- Identify which international agencies and/or international human-rights mechanisms are mandated to respond to such violations or deal with their consequences.

- Clarify the particular responsibilities of your own organisation under these laws and decide on its position in regard to submitting evidence to current or future investigations or proceedings of international or national courts.

Mapping political commitment and resources

Another key part of any protection assessment is to identify who actually, or potentially, has the necessary desire and ability to protect people from the threats they are facing. The ability of a state authority, organisation, community or individual to protect is determined by a mixture of the resources it has available, political attitude and personal conviction. These need to be understood as critical to the context in which you are planning your own protection strategy. The ICRC encapsulates these various resources and characteristics with the phrase 'compliance aptitude' – a mixture of protective will and protective capacity.[8]

This process requires you to examine a range of actors, including the different organs of the relevant state authority; armed forces and armed groups; individual commanders and fighters; war-affected communities and individual victims; other states; multinational companies; and international organisations, humanitarian agencies, and human-rights organisations.

The aim is to understand where protective will exists, where it is being blocked and how best it might be mobilised and supported.

[8] This is a term developed by the ICRC in its detention work.

Working through the checklists in this section will help you to develop an effective situation analysis of the conditions confronting you. The specific mandate or operational focus of your agency will obviously dictate where you concentrate most of your analysis and assessment, in line with your agency's target group and expertise. This process will help to see human suffering in war and disaster in the wider terms of the rights of protected persons, the responsibilities of states, the criminal responsibility of individuals, and the needs, vulnerabilities, and capacities of protected populations themselves.

Checklist G

Protective capability, intent and compliance aptitude

- Identify how key policies of the authorities aim to realise effective protection or not, and whether the practice in the field lives up to the policy espoused in political capitals.

- Gauge the realistic capacity of the political and military actors to provide sufficient and appropriate protection. Identify gaps in resources, including human resources, material, knowledge and expertise that are preventing them from doing so.

- Gauge the willingness of political and military actors to comply with international legal standards. In doing so, also assess their susceptibility to influence – in the form of pressure or support – and identify other valuable individuals and organisations that may not have obvious material resources but may have significant moral authority, willingness to take action and political leverage.

- Identify the positive attributes, such as expertise, previous experience, innovation, courage and effective leadership, among potential protectors that may contribute to their protective ability.

- Map the strengths of, and the gaps in, any network of powerful relationships that may determine the ability of state authorities, humanitarian agencies and vulnerable communities to encourage a strong and positive protection environment. Identify any key individuals particularly responsible for shaping and sustaining such relationships.

2 | 6

section **six**

Step two: setting protection outcomes and objectives

This section moves to the second phase of the project cycle and focuses on programme design. With a completed situation analysis and needs assessment, you are now in a position to define the protection outcomes people urgently need and to set the programme objectives necessary to secure these outcomes.

1 | Situation analysis and protection assessment

2 | Setting protection outcomes and objectives

3 | Choosing protection activities

4 | Monitoring protection outcomes

A clear sense of the desired outcome of any type of protection work is a prerequisite in designing an appropriate programme. Forming a practical vision of what it means for people to be protected in a given situation is critical to an agency's ability to act in the interests of civilian communities. To secure these outcomes, your programme will need a set of clear objectives that identify what you are trying to do. Clear objectives will also enable your agency to monitor and evaluate its protection work from the outset, measuring success and failure, learning from experience and being accountable for its actions.

Setting priorities

A good situation analysis and protection assessment should enable you to prioritise the most pressing violations and threats for your agency to focus on. This process of prioritisation will turn on a judgement of what is most devastating to the people at risk and what is most appropriate and achievable for your agency to address. With an assessment complete, setting programming priorities is best done by answering the following questions.

• **Which violations and threats – primary and secondary – are having the severest impact on individuals and communities?**

• **Which are the most prevalent and persistent?**

• **What are the people's most dangerous vulnerabilities?**

• **Which is our agency best mandated and equipped to address?**

At this point, quick reference to the protection equation risk = threat + vulnerability × time will help you to see clearly where your priorities lie in a given situation by linking specific priorities to each part of the equation.

Once you have agreed your programming priorities, you can set particular protection outcomes that represent a specific and significant reduction in the incidence of violations, the severity of threat, the vulnerability of the population and the level of risk.

Specifying protection outcomes

Specific protection outcomes involve clear changes in the experience, safety and well-being of affected civilian communities. These desired changes are obviously positive and mean a real improvement in people's daily lives. The best protection outcomes are very practical descriptions of achievable changes and improved scenarios for people on the ground. And, of course, they must refer to primary and secondary threats.

Ideally, protection outcomes represent complete solutions to people's suffering but it is important to be realistic in situations of ongoing war or protracted political violence. In many cases, the best outcome a community and an agency may hope for is in fact the least bad outcome rather than the ideal scenario. For example, you may have to accept that your programme cannot end the threats or violations. Instead you have to limit your protection outcomes to reducing the levels of vulnerability faced by the civilian population concerned.

Ideally, however, you will choose to do both in parallel by ending threats and reducing vulnerability. But you can seldom hope to achieve these two goals simultaneously. For example, a swift and adequate food aid programme may take only a few weeks to help communities to reduce their exposure to abduction when farming or searching for food. By contrast, it could take months or years to reduce the level of threat of abduction, through adequate policing and the disarmament of militias.

Box 7

Some examples of protection outcomes

- All people in towns in District X will have sufficient and safe access to food aid until free movement is secured again in the surrounding area.
- All children in IDP camps in District Y will have access to good-quality primary education.
- Young men will have profitable and desirable economic alternatives to militia recruitment. People will have full knowledge of their rights to assistance and protection and be increasingly able to claim them from the responsible authorities without intimidation or discrimination.
- An impartial, efficient and effective mechanism for redressing violations of land rights will be set in motion by the responsible authorities.
- Women and girls will have safe access to water and move freely to collect it without intimidation.
- Families will have sufficient and appropriately designed shelter in IDP camps that enables them to balance privacy with freedom of movement and association.

Setting your objectives

If **protection outcomes** describe what needs to happen for people to lead safer, more dignified lives and to realise their wider social and economic rights, **protection objectives** describe what your programme intends to achieve, whether in the short, medium or long term. Some objectives – like delivering humanitarian assistance or reducing certain immediate risks – can be implemented relatively quickly. Others, like changing military policy, overcoming violent political ideologies, negotiating access or disarming militarised societies, may present deep and long-term structural challenges.

Whether they are immediate or long term, your protection objectives should be **SMART**.

- **S**pecific – it must tell you something particular.

- **M**easurable – it must be able to be aggregated and compared over time.

- **A**chievable – it must be possible to collect and process.

- **R**elevant – it must relate to your outcomes and to all of the different social groups at risk.

- **T**ime-bound – it must refer to particular periods.

Protection objectives should also be framed in terms of an action that describes exactly what you are trying to effect with your protection activities: for example, to stop, prevent, support, change, persuade, mobilise, care for, treat, restore, redress; provide, monitor or report.

Changing behaviour

A great deal of protection work is about changing behaviour. As a result, protection objectives need to be equally precise about who you are targeting – state authorities, armed groups, individuals, communities or other agencies – in your efforts to change the situation. In more detail still, it is important to specify particular departments, offices and individuals in state-authority, agency or armed-group command structure. Be clear about whether you are seeking to change a policy or simply the way it is put into practice.

Most protection objectives are likely to concentrate on three kinds of changes in any given situation: changing the behaviour of perpetrators, changing the actions of responsible authorities, and reducing the vulnerability of affected communities.

Changing the behaviour of perpetrators

This should result in a reduction in the number of casualties, disappearances, forced displacements, threats and other measurable human-rights abuses over time. The particular objectives you agree will depend on your analysis of the situation. For example, if violations against civilians are a deliberate tactic of war, your objective may be to persuade or shame those who are perpetrating these abuses into changing their behaviour or to mobilise more powerful players to coerce them into doing so. If abuses arise because frontline troops 'don't know any better', then your objective may focus on ensuring that command structures are tightened and troops are made aware of their obligations under international humanitarian law. If evidence suggests that people are joining the militias and attacking civilians because it is the only way to make a living, your objective centres on developing alternative livelihoods for vulnerable youth.

A good analysis will also have identified critical permissive attitudes and resources that facilitate violations or make them morally and socially acceptable in the perpetrating organisations. These more structural problems are likely to require longer-term objectives. If the availability of small arms is a major factor, you may have a long-term objective of reducing arms availability. If rape is considered an acceptable spoil of war or is being perpetrated as a deliberate form of ethnic or nationalist domination, then one of your objectives may be to change these attitudes at the same time as reducing the stigma associated with victims of rape.

Changing the actions of responsible authorities

These objectives should result in the development and practical implementation of government or armed-group policies, commitments and actions to reduce violence, displacement and deprivation and to increase civilian protection.

Having identified which authorities have primary responsibility for stopping the perpetrators, halting the violations and increasing humanitarian access, your objectives may centre on persuading government or UN commanders to increase patrols or police protection in vulnerable areas. If members of state forces are engaged in sexual violence and there is no system for reporting and investigating allegations against them, then your objective may be to put such a system in place and monitor its effect.

Government or agency authorities with responsibility for dealing with the consequences of violations and civilian suffering will also need to be targeted in your objectives. If the ministry of the interior has a policy of cutting off assistance to IDPs that results in people being forced back to areas where they are at risk, your objective may be to bring that policy into line with the Guiding Principles on Internal Displacement. If state authorities are unwilling or unable to provide humanitarian assistance to civilian populations, another of your objectives may be to ensure that your agency implements such a programme itself.

Reducing the vulnerability of affected communities

These objectives should aim to support civilian communities so that they can also change their behaviour by choosing safer options in the way they live, move and meet their needs or improve the way they organise politically to challenge the threats against them.

If people are no longer planting crops in outlying fields or travelling to clinics because they are afraid of abduction, then your objective may be to develop alternative, safer livelihoods or to provide food aid and healthcare where people feel safe. Improved water supplies and better site planning in villages and camps could similarly reduce the times and places that people are exposed to risk. If people are afraid to go back to their home villages, your objective may be to ensure that they have access to reliable, impartial information about the conditions in their home areas.

A major objective in your protection work may also involve increasing the organisational capacity of civil society movements and people's organisations by supporting them in their efforts to mobilise popular support for pro-protection policies and society-wide campaigns to end policies of violation and abuse.

Checking your objectives

Once you have identified your objectives, cross-check them to see if, taken together, they can be expected to deliver the desired outcomes. What assumptions are you making about external events, access, resources, influence and the contributions of others? Are they realistic or overly optimistic? Is there anything more you can do, perhaps alone, perhaps with other agencies, to make success more likely?

Most importantly, in any direct programming with vulnerable communities you need to check continuously that your objectives and actions do not result in exposing them to greater risk. In other words, you must ensure that humanitarian assistance programmes (like food distribution, water-points and economic or agricultural asset support) or advocacy work (like representations to belligerent authorities, international media work and campaigning) does not prove counter-protective and put people in new danger of raiding, accelerated military campaigning or collective punishment.

Box 8

Elements of a good protection programme

A good programme of protection:

- enables a significant challenge to be mounted against the violations, abuses and consequences of war and disaster by harnessing to maximum effect the actions of responsible authorities, people's own self-protection capacity, the protective capacity of your own agency and the complementary protective capacity of other organisations. In other words, it is as participatory and complementary as possible.

- is clear about its outcomes – reducing threats or people's vulnerability to those threats – and selects judiciously between the five modes of protective activity: substitution, support to services, mobilisation, persuasion and denunciation.

- is realistic in its assumptions of what your agency can and cannot change in the short, medium and longer terms.

- is complementary with others so that the strategic sum of its parts is sufficient to meet the range of protection needs that people are experiencing.

2 | 7

section **seven**

Step three: choosing protection activities

This section examines the five *modes of action* that are commonly recognised as the main ways in which humanitarian agencies can help to protect people. The first three modes – denunciation, persuasion and mobilisation – are essentially humanitarian advocacy activities. The other two modes of action – capacity-building and substitution – will usually involve combinations of humanitarian assistance and shared technical expertise on the ground.

This section also looks at two other key operational techniques common to all five modes – humanitarian presence and information sharing. This section also introduces the complementarity matrix and gives a case study example of the design of a protection-focused humanitarian programme.

1 | Situation analysis and protection assessment

2 | Setting protection outcomes and objectives

3 | Choosing protection activities

4 | Monitoring protection outcomes

Protection outcomes and objectives set out what you want to happen and what you are going to do to make it happen. It is now necessary to move into the third phase of the project cycle and look at the practical activities that you can implement to meet your objectives and achieve successful protection outcomes.

Plan your activities with endangered communities

But first, before considering those five modes of action, it is important to remember that the first line of defence in protection is often the affected community itself. People targeted by violence or experiencing the physical deprivations of war often play the most critical role in securing their own safety and survival.

It is not always possible to reach the most endangered civilian populations and to plan with them directly and openly. Wherever you have such contact, make sure that your humanitarian assistance programming and advocacy activities support their own self-protection activities. If contact and access are prohibited or logistically impossible, use the best information you have to understand community strategies and to enable them where appropriate.

In your advocacy work, be sure to check whether your agency is best placed to advocate on behalf of those in need of protection or whether your skills are better used to support their own efforts to organise and negotiate their own safety. In all your assistance and advocacy programming, keep checking that what you are providing or what you are saying is genuinely supportive and not becoming counter-protective by exposing people to new risks or leading to a reduction of humanitarian access and activity by increasingly resistant authorities.

Modes of action

There are five main modes of action that you can use to meet the protection objectives you have identified. The first three (*Denunciation*, *Persuasion* and *Mobilisation*) do not involve humanitarian assistance but are differing means of applying pressure to ensure the compliance and cooperation of the relevant authorities in line with standards of civilian protection laid down in international law.

The fourth and fifth modes are ways of providing direct practical assistance or expertise to civilian communities faced with violations, threats and their social and economic consequences. *Capacity building* is appropriate where responsible authorities and communities are willing to take action but simply do not have the means. *Substitution* is a last resort, but will frequently be necessary when the responsible authorities are unwilling or manifestly incapable, despite support, of taking appropriate action. Substitution sees a humanitarian agency taking the operational place of responsible authorities.

Your choice of mode in a given situation will be determined by the following considerations:

- **the willingness of the authorities to respond themselves**

- **the capacity of authorities to respond**

- **the capacity of civilian communities to help themselves**

- **your agency's capacity to respond**

- **the political risk of different modes for the security of the civilian population**

- **the political risk of different modes for the security and access of your own agency**

- **the duration of your action**

- **your experience from previous similar actions in this setting**

- **what other are choosing to do.**

In other words, you must choose judiciously between modes on the basis of what you are trying to achieve on the ground, who you need to influence to make it happen and what risks you might run for yourself and others in the process.

The ability and willingness of the responsible authorities to protect civilian communities will always be a critical factor in your choice of mode and the programme you design. More negative authorities are likely to require the more coercive strategies of denunciation and mobilisation, while more positive authorities may respond to the more collaborative and cooperative modes of persuasion, substitution and support to services. But do not assume this stereotype. Humanitarian agencies have often found important groups of pro-protection allies within a negative and resistant authority whom they can mobilise and support. Similarly, positive but incompetent authorities often respond best to denunciation when they fail to make the most of the support on offer.

Your choice of operational mode will also be determined by your particular objective: whether it is to change the behaviour of the perpetrators, to influence responsible authorities or to reduce the vulnerability of the communities to threats. If direct provision of services is a priority, you may well play down coercive modes to seek access for substitution programmes.

Figure opposite
Modes of action in protection

Source: adapted from Bonard, P (1999) Modes of Action used by Humanitarian Players: Criteria for Operational Complementarity. Geneva: ICRC.

Modes of Action

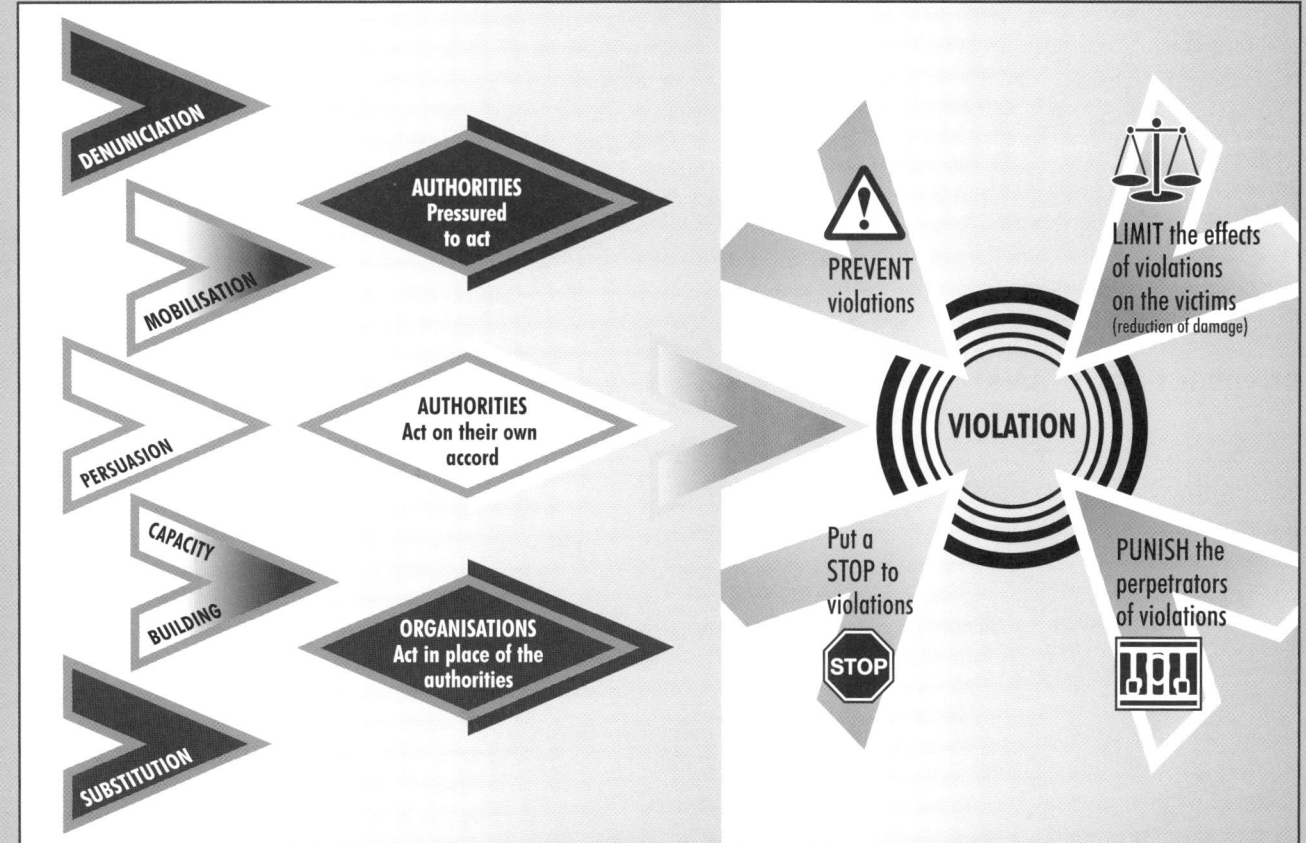

1 Denunciation is pressuring authorities through public disclosure into meeting their obligations and protecting individuals or groups exposed to abuse.

2 Mobilisation is sharing information in a discreet way with selected people, bodies or states that have the capacity to influence the authorities to satisfy their obligations and to protect individuals and groups exposed to violations. This is likely to involve mobilising actors at different levels — high-level state authorities, civil society and communities. The choice of partners in any mobilisation strategy is critical.

3 Persuasion is convincing the authorities through further private dialogue to fulfil their obligations and to protect individuals and groups exposed to violations.

4 Capacity building is giving support to existing national and/or local structures to enable them to carry out their functions to protect individuals and groups.

5 Substitution is directly providing services or material assistance to people in need of protection.

Humanitarian advocacy

Advocacy is a core area of protective practice for both humanitarian and human-rights agencies. It is about convincing decision-makers to change. Persuasion, mobilisation and denunciation are different types of advocacy. Any one of these approaches can operate on a spectrum that uses hard or soft messages, collaborative or confrontational postures, private or public pressure. Advocacy is a skill that is required at all levels of protective action from the most local encounter to the grandest political arena. It encompasses everything from persuading the village chief to allocate land to displaced families to influencing a senior General on the conduct of his army.[9]

Advocacy objectives

Your most immediate advocacy objectives may be to bring pressure on responsible authorities to ensure that people's basic needs for protection and assistance are met. Here you are likely to need quick results from key decision-makers.

More long-term advocacy objectives will also be important to ensure continuing protection. Here you may need to focus on a broader range of institutional targets. Key decision-makers play a crucial role in bringing about change. But they cannot do it alone. For change to be sustained, a reformed environment and infrastructure is needed which outlasts individual decision-makers and their interest in a particular issue. Alongside advocacy strategies for immediate prevention or remedy of violations and threats, a long-term protection programme is also likely to require environment-building advocacy. This is a deeper, more structural process that challenges society as a whole by aiming to change policy, laws, attitudes, beliefs, behaviour and institutions.

Advocating for new policies and institutions may include calls for establishing new legal structures and rules by which violent behaviour is controlled. This might involve more organised adherence to the Geneva Conventions, human-

[9] See Mancini-Griffoli, Deborah and Andre Picot (2004) *Humanitarian Negotiation: a Handbook for Securing Access, Assistance and Protection for Civilians in Armed Conflict.* Geneva: Centre for Humanitarian Dialogue.

rights law and refugee law by states and armed groups alike. Realising this might involve successful calls for improved procedures for investigation, prosecution and imprisonment.

Beyond policies and institutions, advocacy needs to be aimed at broader targets still so that changes can be made in widespread attitudes and beliefs that drive and legitimise violations in war and disaster. Advocacy aimed at building a more moral and legal environment in a war-torn society is thus a challenge that runs deep. It will involve pressure to establish more humane political values, improvements in law and legal practice, the training of security forces, and the development of an increasingly non-violent public culture.

Different types of advocacy require different levels of agency resources. Depending on the resources of your agency, you may be limited in the type of advocacy that you can conduct. However, resources are not the only factor in successful advocacy: courage, passion, organisation and determination count for a lot. With support, even the smallest community-based organisations have managed to achieve remarkable results. Nevertheless, a small health agency working on its own, for example, is unlikely to be able to mount and sustain a massive media-based campaign.

The mandate of your agency will also determine the nature of your advocacy. One of the ICRC's great strengths is its ability to sustain long-term relationships and work progressively to achieve change, but its rigorous neutrality makes it unlikely that it will pursue hard, public denunciations of violating parties on a regular basis.

Advocacy as persuasion

Decision-makers need to be convinced of the need for change and of their own need to act to make that change. Persuasion tends to use the force of argument rather than the argument of force to convince appropriate authorities to protect civilians.

Box 10

Negotiating for IDP rights

In the Uraba region of Colombia, internally displaced persons (IDPs) fleeing violence and seeking shelter in nearby towns initially encountered hostile or indifferent attitudes from local political and military authorities that blocked their movement to safer areas and consistently pressured them to leave the towns and return home. Supported by Colombian Catholic Groups and NGOs, displaced community leaders organised a series of formal meetings with government authorities to make known their needs, request assistance and seek government guarantees before they would consider return. These meetings took the form of official bilateral negotiations and typically ended with signed agreements about a range of rights.

Source: Inter-Agency Standing Committee (2002) *Growing the Sheltering Tree: Protecting Rights through Humanitarian Action, Programmes and Practices Gathered from the Field.* Geneva: Inter-Agency Standing Committee, p 74.

Reasonable arguments must be presented in the terms most likely to convince a particular decision-maker. The right line of argument may not be the one that would persuade most humanitarians. Instead, an effective argument is more likely to be one that is consistent with the decision-maker's moral view of the world and self-interest.[10] While it is important to be principled in your argument according to your organisation's values and beliefs, you should express yourself in ways that will make most immediate sense to those you are trying to convince. Persuasion can be undertaken through a variety of approaches including face-to-face meetings, targeted reports, letters or formal delegations.

Advocacy as mobilisation

Making an argument together with others usually results in a more forceful case. Mobilisation is the art of building, informing and energising an appropriate network of powerful decision-makers into a particular form of action to protect civilians.

Mobilisation can take many forms. In a bottom-up form, it may involve the support and mobilisation of in-country civil society organisations in favour of affected populations. For example, some of the most powerful organisations in protracted warfare in parts of Latin America have been well-organised solidarity movements of civilians *for* civilians. Internationally, a wide-ranging coalition of people can come together to argue the same point in many countries. In a more top-down manifestation, it may be a matter of catching key people's attention and engaging their commands. For example, sometimes a single telephone call to the right decision-maker at the right moment from the right person can mobilise a powerful network of local, national and international resources. Often, mobilisation requires both approaches working simultaneously.

[10] See Mancini-Griffoli, Deborah and Andre Picot (2004) *Humanitarian Negotiation: a Handbook for Securing Access, Assistance and Protection for Civilians in Armed Conflict.* Geneva: Centre for Humanitarian Dialogue.

Box 11

Getting the message out

For many days, Pikit was effectively isolated from the rest of the world. Communication lines were cut. At the parish compound, we were saved by an old generator that powered our Globelines battery-charger. Our telephone line was the town's only access to the media, and we made extensive use of it. It was busy with in-coming calls from NDBC radio stations. My idea was to report everything that I saw and heard so that the outside world would know what was happening inside the town of Pikit. Blow by blow, radio stations aired our reports from Pikit until NGOs and government authorities heard and took notice of our plight. It was only then that we ended our isolation.

Source: Fr Roberto Layson, OMI, in *In War, the Real Enemy is War itself,* Initiatives for International Dialogue. Davao City: Philippines, p 23.

Advocacy as denunciation

The logic of denunciation is to shame decision-makers into taking particular actions through public exposure, private conscience or obvious interest. Although this can be an effective type of intervention, it can sometimes be highly confrontational and close the door to more constructive relationships in the future. Therefore, it should be used with caution.

Because of this, denunciation is usually portrayed as the last resort in humanitarian advocacy. But this need not be the case. In some situations denunciation is a natural first resort. Some atrocities are so terrible that they require instant and loud denunciation. In some situations the authorities tolerate denunciation or have no choice but to accept it, and so it can be run in parallel with effective access and field programmes. And denunciation need not always be loud and public. It can also be private, quiet and carefully targeted.

Checklist H

Humanitarian advocacy

- Ensure that your advocacy is impartial, based objectively on real violations and threats, targets the right actors and is well timed.
- Put a very high value on the accuracy and credibility of the information on which you base your advocacy campaign. Look respectable and be authoritative when you present your case in private and in public.
- Protect your sources – both among your staff and within the local community – and work on the principle of informed consent with regard to statements that you intend to make. People concerned need to approve how and when you use their words and experience.
- Recognise a possible trade-off between humanitarian access and humanitarian advocacy and involve your staff and the communities that you are trying to protect in such decisions.
- Ask what role your agency can play to give civilian communities the voice they need to change the decisions that affect their lives. Can you use your position of influence to bring them into meetings and discussions? Think how you could use your resources to build networks of community groups so that collectively they can have a stronger voice.
- Judge carefully when loud or quiet advocacy strategies are best and, as appropriate, apply different types of pressure to different kinds of targets on different levels.

Humanitarian assistance

Humanitarian assistance is perhaps the most familiar form of activity for most humanitarian agencies. It is essentially about providing humanitarian services and commodities either directly (substitution), or more indirectly via the supply of advice or resources through a local authority or partner organisation (support to services). In simple terms, humanitarian assistance is about giving aid in the form of material and expertise.

This kind of humanitarian action meets many of the most pressing needs of people by protecting them from the extremes of hunger, thirst, disease, destitution, family separation, total poverty and indignity. As such, it helps to realise a large number of the rights set out in international legal standards.

Although not all assistance can provide protection from further violence and abuses, assistance and protection are intimately linked, as material assistance can be both protective and endangering in certain situations.

Assistance as an entry point to protection

Assistance programmes can provide an excellent entry point for agencies to engage in protection work. In some situations, the presence of an agency on the ground in a predominantly assistance mode enables it to become more aware of potential patterns of abuse or particular violations taking place in the surrounding area. In this way, assistance programmes can provide a starting point from which to design and operate protection programmes.

Protective assistance

But the link does not stop there. Assistance itself can also protect people. Your protection objectives can dictate the best type of assistance to provide and when and where to deliver it. Used creatively, with clear protection outcomes in mind, humanitarian aid can double up as *risk-limiting assistance*.

Box 12

Mobile clinics providing healthcare and protection monitoring

In Sri Lanka, the deterioration of the health infrastructure, the wide dispersal of displaced people, poor transport and chronic insecurity made it difficult for IDPs to access adequate healthcare. UNICEF and its programme partners responded by supporting mobile health clinics that moved with IDPs and travelled to areas where they were concentrated, to provide basic diagnostic, curative and referral services. At the same time, these mobile health teams were also able to assess and report on the wider protection needs of the population.

Source: Inter-Agency Standing Committee (2002) *Growing the Sheltering Tree: Protecting Rights through Humanitarian Action, Programmes and Practices Gathered from the Field.* Geneva: Inter-Agency Standing Committee, p 118.

Providing humanitarian aid like food, water, shelter and healthcare can protect people from further deprivation and violence by reducing immediate risks. But beyond this it can also prevent them from being forced to adopt survival strategies that expose them to new secondary risks. For example, people may live in an area where there is an abundant supply of water but many dangers in collecting and carrying it. Shortage of water is not the problem but the dangerous location of water-points is. New wells dug in safer areas that lessen the risk of dangerous journeys are a classic example of a humanitarian assistance activity responding to a protection objective. This is risk-limiting assistance at its best. Similarly, developing alternative livelihoods and siting services closer to where people live can stop people from having to resort to prostitution or dangerous patterns of movement to collect firewood or seek medicine, for example. Adequate food supply in displaced camps can remove the risk of people returning home to try and plant their fields while fighting and violence continues.

Assistance-related risks

But, paradoxically, assistance can endanger people too. Your protection objectives must also help to inform how you provide assistance without exposing people to new assistance-related threats. This may mean ensuring that water distribution points are well lit and not in isolated areas, to reduce the risk of assault, and ensuring that new wells have fair ownership systems that do not leave people open to exploitation by cliques charging extortionate prices for safe water. Or, it may mean distributing cooked meals rather than dry rations because of a real threat that the recipients will be robbed and hurt as soon as they leave the distribution point.

Box 13

Renovating an urban water system to limit the risk of shootings

During the war in Bosnia and Herzegovena in 1995, IRC developed a water project in Sarajevo to prevent people from having to go to the river or stand in long, slow queues to collect water from trucks where they were exposed to sniper and artillery fire. The water project ingeniously used very old water pipelines that were renovated to get water to areas better protected from military attack. This water project played a key role in enabling the safe collection of clean water when the external supply to the city was completely cut off by the Bosnian Serb military laying siege to the city throughout the summer.

Source: Inter-Agency Standing Committee (2002) *Growing the Sheltering Tree: Protecting Rights through Humanitarian Action, Programmes and Practices Gathered from the Field.* Geneva: Inter-Agency Standing Committee, p 115.

Finally, protection can dictate when not to provide assistance at all. If the main way that a community stays safe in a conflict is by avoiding drawing attention to itself, people may well be safer if they are not descended upon by humanitarian agencies with relief supplies and other high-value commodities worth raiding.

There are many specific guidelines on humanitarian assistance in the Sphere standards and other good-practice texts but the following checklist highlights some key points about the protective value of humanitarian assistance.

Checklist 1

Humanitarian assistance

- Never put together a team of protection specialists only, but ensure that you have a majority of assistance experts who can work to see protection needs and protection solutions in the round.
- Humanitarian assistance programmes responding to current violations or remedying past abuses are best designed with a protective edge that consciously tries to reduce current threats and prevent future violations.
- Health, water, shelter or livelihood programmes are best designed with people's protection from violence in mind. All humanitarian aid programmes need to 'think protection' and focus on ways in which assistance programming in all sectors can reduce people's vulnerability to other forms of attack, violation, coercion, cooption or deprivation.
- Humanitarian assistance programmes should be scrutinised continuously to ensure that they are not becoming counter-protective in any way by putting people in new danger or at further risk via some form of protection paradox.
- In the way that they are designed and managed, humanitarian assistance programmes should be respectful of the wider rights of protected persons enshrined in human-rights law, international humanitarian law and refugee law, including freedom of expression and freedom of religion.
- Wherever possible, use humanitarian assistance programmes to disseminate humanitarian law, human rights law and the Code of Conduct and include humanitarian values and principles in educational programmes.

Presence and accompaniment

The physical presence of national and international humanitarian workers on the ground close to suffering and threatened communities is a common feature of most humanitarian assistance programmes and the monitoring and witnessing necessary to inform humanitarian advocacy work. This presence can be consciously used to protect people by inhibiting abusive behaviour.

Civilians and humanitarian workers have frequently testified that the presence of humanitarian workers can restrain some acts of violence and increase local sensitivity to international norms and concerns. Several organisations have developed sophisticated methodologies to maximise the protective impact of targeted presence in a variety of distinct conflict situations.[11]

Strategic use of presence is designed simultaneously to affect perceptions and change behaviours of potential abusers, through a series of tactics that involve public visibility, direct accompaniment of threatened parties or communities, diplomatic contact with abusers and authorities, and confidence building and security support for victim communities and sectors. Potential abusers can be dissuaded from attacking civilians by an international presence for a variety of reasons. These include:

• **fear of international pressure or sanction**

• **fear of witnesses and evidence that could lead to future prosecution**

• **concern for their local reputation which can be enhanced by good relations with the international community**

• **concern about embarrassing their superiors**

• **individual moral concern about being seen to commit crimes.**

[11] Most notably Peace Brigades International; see Mahony, Liam and Luis-Enrique Eguren (1997) *Unarmed Bodyguards: International Accompaniment for the Protection of Human Rights.* West Hartford: Kumarian Press.

Box 14

Preventing forcible displacement

In Sri Lanka in 1993, a paramilitary force threatened to close down an IDP camp by expelling all IDPs and destroying the camp. At the request of the local IDP organisation, Peace Brigades International (PBI) sent two observers to the camp. They arrived early and placed themselves at the entrance to the camp, in a clearly visible position. Some local journalists also turned up as well. They waited for several hours until two vehicles with people in military uniform arrived. They entered the camp shouting but their attitude changed when they saw the international observers and the local press. After a tense meeting with the IDPs in the camp, the paramilitaries left, visibly angry and threatening that they would be back to evict the IDPs once and for all. They never came back.

Source: Inter-Agency Standing Committee (2002) *Growing the Sheltering Tree: Protecting Rights through Humanitarian Action, Programmes and Practices Gathered from the Field.* Geneva: Inter-Agency Standing Committee, p 171.

Protective accompaniment is a specific strategy that has been developed in human-rights practice to protect particularly threatened individuals, organisations and communities by providing them with a visible international presence – sometimes sporadic and sometimes around the clock. The presence can dissuade attacks and encourage the accompanied people to carry out their important tasks as leaders or activists in a threatened community. Accompaniment is, therefore, a specific form of a long-term and highly targeted presence that can be part of a wider process of support for, and mobilisation of, civil society groups or mandated agencies, which increases the pressure on authorities or armed groups.

Mere presence itself cannot guarantee safety for anyone, and any strategy that uses presence must carefully analyse the political situation to judge how local actors will react to a humanitarian presence. Presence must also always be used in the context of a broader protection strategy that involves other assistance or advocacy interventions. Given that humanitarian workers are sometimes targeted for attack themselves, difficult judgements must be made on how much relative protection a certain presence might offer set against the immediate risks to humanitarians and the potential backlash risk it presents to communities. However, used carefully and strategically, humanitarian presence can sometimes be a very effective form of protection in itself.

Box 15

Accompaniment of relief supplies

The physical accompaniment of medical supplies to their destination may require that medical coordinators become shipping and transport agents as well. In the case of the Palestinian Self-Rule Areas, the WHO special coordinator spent many hours physically on the receiving dock getting medical emergency kits cleared through security and customs, and then transporting them in WHO vehicles through roadblocks to cut-off communities. The physical presence of WHO medical officers not only ensured that the supplies reached the Palestinian communities in need, but offered powerful reassurance to the Israeli authorities that the goods were truly humanitarian.

Source: Inter-Agency Standing Committee (2002) *Growing the Sheltering Tree: Protecting Rights through Humanitarian Action, Programmes and Practices Gathered from the Field.* Geneva: Inter-Agency Standing Committee, p 122.

To date, most humanitarian agencies have not thought deeply and strategically about presence or accompaniment as an explicit humanitarian tactic. But there are now a number of good-practice principles emerging around the use of presence and accompaniment as a humanitarian tactic that can be adapted and applied by a variety of agencies with presence on the ground in order to achieve better protection outcomes.

Accompaniment can be used to protect particular people in a particular place or along a particular route or to accompany particular commodities through a difficult environment.

Box 16

Never giving up: Hungary, 1944

Even in the most extreme situations of war and genocide, the best humanitarians never give up trying to protect people. Their determination to save even one life means that they keep having new ideas, trying new tactics and using the power of their personality to bluff, persuade or outwit those violating and abusing people. Most of these humanitarian heroes remain unremembered but occasionally their story comes to light. In Hungary in 1944, Friedrich Born (an ICRC delegate) and Raol Wallenberg (a Swedish diplomat) combined personal courage, innovation and charisma to work determinedly with the Vatican's Papal Nuncio, Angelo Rotta, the Swiss Consul, Carl Lutz, and a few other diplomats to protect Hungarian Jews from forced marches and concentration camps. They issued important-looking letters of protection to stall the Hungarian authorities and gathered people into safe houses which they protected actively with their presence and international authority — Born's Hungarian assistant noting that: 'everybody knew Born, this was part of his success'.

Finally, even in the midst of failure as the Nazis and their Hungarian allies led thousands of Jewish people on vicious 15-day death marches on which thousands of people died of exhaustion or were clubbed to death by their guards, Born and Wallenberg stayed with the marchers, driving up and down the column with a mobile clinic and trucks to try to rescue as many as they could. Born also took 4000 metres of film of these marches which he sent out of the country to alert others. In the particular conditions of Hungary, there was opportunity for action of this kind. Born, Wallenberg and others saw the opportunity and never stopped trying to protect people, saving several thousand people as a result.

Source: Moorehead, Caroline (1998) *Dunant's Dream: War, Switzerland and the History of the Red Cross.* Harper Collins, pp 445–454.

Checklist J

Humanitarian presence and accompaniment

- Ensure that your presence is considered and that you understand how it is perceived, valued or feared by protected persons, authorities and potential violators alike. All of these actors will have different and often conflicting interests in your presence in a given situation and will seek to use it or abuse it accordingly.

- Recognise how your presence can function as an asset or a liability and use or withdraw it consciously in a preconceived, deliberate and targeted manner.

- Use your personality carefully to project the appropriate attitude and character in a given situation. This might vary between: observation and a relatively reserved form of quiet power; a friendly, open and sympathetic air; a more explicit role as a witness; or determination and confrontation and the clear projection of internationally mandated authority.

- Use presence deliberately as targeted protective diplomacy by keeping in regular contact with local authorities or other leaders who have influence over abusers, in order to ensure that they are constantly considering international presence and witness in the cost-benefit calculations governing their political and military choices.

- Develop a certain style of diplomatic discourse that internationalises local protection issues and gives them significant international weight without sounding too pompous. Use this nuanced but diplomatic way of talking about protection to communicate with key actors in a way that makes them think as often as possible about the political implications of being observed by the international community.

- Where appropriate, combine a targeted proactive presence around specific hotspots and persons with a less routine, widespread and mobile presence that gives potential violators and protected persons the feeling that you are 'always around'.

- Target your presence to get close to particular groups of vulnerable people at particular high-risk moments and in high-risk places. With limited resources, your presence should focus on protecting the key groupings of the civilian population that are most in danger.

- Where appropriate, develop a committed strategy of deploying international observers. But remember that simply being there does not provide protection. An international protective presence requires a strategy behind it that focuses on detailed observation and active dissuasion of human-rights and humanitarian violations. Also remember that international observers are effective only in conflicts where the parties are responsive to international pressure.

- Wherever possible and appropriate, use your project sites (clinics, water-points, offices, food distribution centres and schools) as safe places for individuals particularly at risk.

Information as protection

The importance of information in any type of successful protection work cannot be underestimated. Information can save lives and is very much two-way between civilian communities and humanitarian agencies. As we have seen already, information that passes from affected civilian communities to humanitarian workers can help agencies to understand how people are suffering and coping, so informing and guiding the appropriate design of protection and assistance programmes.

Important information on violations and unacceptable conditions can also be shared still further with responsible authorities and mandated or specialist protection agencies like the ICRC, the UN High Commissioner for Human Rights, UNHCR, UNOCHA and UNICEF. How openly or discreetly humanitarian agencies share this information requires a judgement in each particular context. Likewise, how the organisations in receipt of such information protect their sources and act on the information most effectively must be given equal consideration.

Equally important, and more easily overlooked, is the important practical information that can be passed from humanitarian agencies to the civilian population or between civilian communities with a humanitarian agency as intermediary. Giving people access to impartial information from a source they trust can help communities and individuals to protect themselves and stay in touch.

People caught up in violent conflict make calculated decisions all the time about the relative risks of the often dangerous options and dilemmas that are open to them: to stay at home or to flee, to plant crops or to hide the seeds, to join the militia or to stay out of the conflict. These decisions are made on the

Box 17

Information and advice on land rights

In Georgia, UNHCR carried out a comprehensive study of housing and restitution issues facing returnees and displaced people. The study clarified the dimensions of land tenure problems and offered constitutional and legal options for their resolution. UNHCR then supported a network of jurists to provide advice and counselling to displaced persons on property and related matters.

Source: Inter-Agency Standing Committee (2002) *Growing the Sheltering Tree: Protecting Rights through Humanitarian Action, Programmes and Practices Gathered from the Field.* Geneva: Inter-Agency Standing Committee, p 148.

best information available to them – information that is frequently incomplete and inaccurate because of restrictions on their movement or because it is deliberately manipulated for political reasons.

What is waiting for me if I return home, and if I stay here what will happen to the camp? What legal right do I have to compensation for the loss of my land and how do I go about exercising it? Am I entitled to any assistance and who should I contact to get it? Information that can answer these questions can be critical to the safety of civilian communities as well as to their economic, social and emotional well-being. It is likely to be of the following main kinds:

• **simple technical information around health or livelihood issues**

• **practical bulletins for IDPs and refugees about the safety situation in areas to which they may be considering a return**

• **tracing information about family members**

• **important information about people's rights under national and international law.**

Much of this information can be vital to affected communities but, if they are left unsupported, such information can also endanger them further in some cases. For example, IDP committees which were set up by humanitarian agencies to alert IDPs to their rights and help them organise to engage more effectively with authorities worked well at the outset, with international guidance and cover. They backfired when the international presence left the area, and the leaders of the committees were arrested and detained. It is essential to discuss the risks involved in knowing and arguing for one's rights with certain authorities so as to gain community consent for such risks and develop ways to mitigate them.

Box 18

Mobile family communications units

In Kosovo, ICRC set up a Family Communications System of 10 mobile units that travelled throughout the province and were each equipped with satellite and mobile phones. Their arrival in towns and villages was announced in advance on the radio. People were able to make telephone calls to contact or find out about missing family members and to share information about their conditions and needs. Other people also filled out the traditional written Red Cross messages or registered their names on ICRC's Family Links website. ICRC worked closely with volunteers in all communities they visited to reach the maximum number of people.

Source: Inter-Agency Standing Committee (2002) *Growing the Sheltering Tree: Protecting Rights through Humanitarian Action, Programmes and Practices Gathered from the Field.* Geneva: Inter-Agency Standing Committee, p 109.

Using the complementarity matrix

A good way to check on the coverage and design of your own humanitarian programme and how it fits within the wider efforts and activities of the international and national protection system is to use the complementarity matrix below.

Using the various boxes in the matrix, you can tick off the kinds of activities being applied, and by whom, around particular protection needs in a situation. This helps to reveal gaps where activities remain untried, and can get you and others thinking more creatively about who could do more, where and how. The matrix can be especially useful as a tool for mapping agency activities in interagency protection meetings. It can also serve as a useful tool in monitoring protection-focused work, which is the subject of the next section.

	Denunciation	Persuasion	Mobilisation	Capacity-building	Substitution
Responsive action					
Remedial action					
Environment-building action					

Example: programme design using protection objectives

Humanitarian agencies commonly work in countries where there is a civil war between various armed groups and the central government. This example of a protection-focused programme is written from the perspective of a humanitarian agency with a history of working in rural areas in such a context. It is perhaps worth noting that many objectives and activities, carried out over different timeframes, may be required to deliver a single outcome. Likewise, although activities and objectives can contribute to several outcomes, their impact is likely to be greatest if these strategic links are made early, at the design stage.

Overall protection aim:

To work with responsible authorities, mandated agencies and the population in need to reduce the incidence of attacks on civilians by *all* parties to the conflict, and to reduce the impact of the attacks on health, access to food and economic security by enabling the free movement of the civilian population and access by humanitarian agencies.

Background

Rival armed groups are carrying out vicious and indiscriminate attacks on rural populations in their respective territories in the north of Country K. Both sides are avoiding attacking each other's forces and are instead deliberately directing their violence against villages and market towns with populations predominantly consisting of civilians from the opposing group.

The violence is characterised by the public killing of village elders, the segregation and disappearance of young men, and extensive sexual violence against young girls and women of all ages. Young men are rounded up in early-morning raids on villages; houses are often burnt down; and food and valuables are pillaged. By day, groups of women are sometimes raped and even abducted when working in the fields, going to market, or collecting water and firewood. This is leading to severe food and water shortages and increasing impoverishment.

These attacks are rapidly curtailing the movement of rural civilians. Young men are forced to flee and limited water sources are under pressure, as women will not leave their villages to access wells. Insecurity on the roads has raised transport prices tenfold, with a significant effect on people's livelihood and survival.

Government forces in the area are trying to intercept and engage all armed groups but the state forces are mainly situated in market towns. These towns are now taking on the characteristics of garrison towns, as government soldiers levy food from the local population, tax goods moving in and out of the town and sexually exploit young women. At present, humanitarian access to the area is sporadic and confined to government-controlled towns.

Protection Outcome One

The civilian population has sufficient food supply, regular and safe access to its fields and markets and sufficient clean water.

Protection objectives
- Ensure that government forces increase the deployment of troops in rural areas, along trading routes and in market towns.
- Encourage leaders of all the armed factions to denounce violence against the civilian population and take appropriate action against the responsible members of their groups.
- Ensure deployment of international military observers to Country K to investigate allegations of attacks on civilians, reporting back to faction leaders and the international community.
- Secure humanitarian agency access to rural communities in order to provide safe water-points and an interim food aid programme within the perimeter of the villages.
- Develop complementary programming with other agencies to meet the above objectives.

Protection activities
- Negotiate agency access with authorities to improve over-used water-points and to develop safer new ones in villages where violence is preventing people from enjoying safe access to sufficient clean water.
- Negotiate access with authorities to carry out a nutritional survey, bring food aid into the relative safety of the villages and distribute it impartially on the basis of need.

- Work with mandated agencies to encourage the ministries of defence and the interior to deploy troops, particularly on market days.
- Persuade the UN to deploy military observers to Country K via in-country alliance building and advocacy work, as well as through the international media.
- Mobilise the in-country diplomatic community to pressure leaders of armed factions into curtailing violence against civilians.

Protection indicators
- Improved nutritional and public health data.
- Observation of, and reported trends in, land cultivation.
- Price and availability of manufactured and agricultural goods in market towns; price of transportation to and from the towns.
- Figures on number of attacks on villages and women.
- Level of confidence and sense of safety among all sections of rural civilian population.
- Number of water-points visited and repaired by agency.

Protection Outcome Two

Young women live free from the threat of sexual exploitation by government forces in garrison towns.

Protection objectives

- Stop troops serving in garrison towns from exploiting vulnerable women and girls.
- Ensure commanders in garrison towns take effective action to prevent sexual exploitation and abuse, and punish those responsible.
- Secure access for victims of sexual violence and abuse to appropriate care and assistance.
- Ensure vulnerable people living in garrison towns receive sufficient humanitarian assistance to prevent the need to resort to prostitution to survive.
- Develop complementary programming with other agencies to meet the above objectives.

Protection activities

- Support a local civil society organisation to document systematically allegations of sexual exploitation within garrison towns and convey this information with the local population, mandated agencies and authorities.
- Pressurise national government authorities into investigating incidents and disciplining troops when appropriate.
- Encourage and support the government to include appropriate military training on the protection of women.
- Launch a public campaign in garrison towns to raise awareness and to de-stigmatise discussion of sexual violence and exploitation.
- Support civil society groups in garrison towns in their efforts to pressure local commanders into controlling and disciplining troops.
- Persuade specialised national and international agencies working on the protection of women and children to develop programmes to support victims of sexual exploitation and violence.
- Persuade donor governments and humanitarian agencies to increase the supply of aid to garrison towns.

Protection indicators

- Reported trends in incidents of sexual exploitation and rape.
- Incidence of specific military training on the protection of women.
- Attitudes of garrison troops to sexual exploitation and violence.
- Existence of an open public debate on the issue.
- Sense of safety among young women in garrison towns.
- Quantity of aid supplied to garrison towns.

Protection Outcome Three

Young men are able to live safely in their villages and to contribute to their family livelihood.

Protection objectives

* Reduce the number of young men abducted and forced into military service.
* Ensure the safe return of young men who have fled to the towns.
* Ensure the safe return of young men who have been abducted.
* Enable young men to carry out economic activities (such as farming and trading) in safety.
* Develop complementary programming with other agencies to meet the above objectives.

Protection activities

* Work with civil society groups or mandated agencies to document disappearances.
* Present all parties to the conflict with lists of the disappeared, and persuade them to investigate and respond.
* Launch a public campaign to highlight the plight of those abducted by armed groups in order to 'shame' those responsible and to encourage them to stop.

Protection indicators

* Trends in the numbers of young men observed living in or returning to villages.
* Take-up of the issue of disappearances by responsible authorities and influential agencies.

2 | 8

section **eight**

Step four: monitoring protection outcomes

This section gives some general guidance on monitoring and evaluating protection programmes. It uses the approach of the previous sections to emphasise the importance of monitoring the situation as it develops and keeping your programme focused on clear protection outcomes and objectives throughout. It introduces the ideas of impact and verifiable protection indicators as the key instrument with which to gauge successes and failures in protection work.

| 1 | Situation analysis and protection assessment | 2 | Setting protection outcomes and objectives | 3 | Choosing protection activities | 4 | Monitoring protection outcomes |

Well-organised programme monitoring offers the vital first line of learning about what works and what does not work in particular protection activities. It is therefore essential that you set up a monitoring system of some kind to gauge the effectiveness of your programme on the ground. This system should be as sensitive as conditions allow and use the best possible indicators to report on the protection outcomes you have set yourself.

While recognising that monitoring is essential, it is also important to acknowledge that monitoring in situations of war and widespread human-rights violations is often extremely difficult. When access, security and resources are a constant challenge, it can be a major achievement just to get something done. To know how well it was done (efficiency), how much has changed (impact) and how far these changes are due to your agency's own actions (attribution) can be extremely difficult to gauge. But it is vital to try.

Depending on how much your objectives are responsive, remedial or environmental, a good monitoring process will need to capture short-term and long-term trends if it is going to measure the impact of protection work accurately.

People-centred monitoring

The best monitoring will be people-centred. It will capture tangible and significant changes in people's daily lives over time. The key question to shape your monitoring might be: **how much is what we are doing, and encouraging others to do, helping to keep people safe, to preserve their personal dignity and integrity and to realise their economic, social and cultural rights?**

Answering this question requires that you constantly monitor two main variables:

1 **the changing nature of the threats and violations ranged against the particular population (the situation)**

2 **people's experience of your strategy and activities (the results of your agency's actions).**

This means taking the collection and analysis of protection indicators seriously, regularly reporting on what you find, and, wherever possible, involving protected persons in the process.

Involving responsible authorities

While every effort needs to be made to involve people in need of protection in any monitoring process, wherever possible you should also try to involve the responsible authorities or abusing parties as well. Actively engaging them in protection monitoring, or at least being able to meet them to discuss your findings, is a vital way of holding them accountable. However, the usual risks apply when sharing information with authorities and others responsible for violations and abuses: do so only if it is not likely to generate a backlash against the community and individuals concerned.

Staff-centred monitoring

Agency personnel are also a valuable source of monitoring information. Staff can be vital for informal monitoring and adapting particular strategies in accordance with certain key questions about improvement. How is the presence of the agency best projected? What kind of advocacy seems to be working? How can aid be more protective? What should we do more of? What should we do less of? What new things might be worth trying?

Regular team meetings provide the best forum in which to monitor in this way. And a good team meeting is one in which all members of staff feel able to share their experience, while knowing that they will be listened to properly. Such meetings can seem hard to prioritise in extreme conditions but they are very important and occasionally eye-opening in what they reveal.

An outsider's perspective

The opinions of experts and agencies outside your organisation are also vitally important in assessing your approach. How you are seen may not be how you see yourself. Soliciting the views of individuals outside your organisation, and views from beyond the civilian communities you are trying to protect, can offer valuable insight into what you are doing well and what you are not doing so well.

Outcome indicators

The key to effective monitoring is the choice of illustrative and collectable indicators. These are signs, statistics or perceptions that can show clearly the status of people's safety and well-being against the outcomes you are trying to achieve. Depending on your precise protection outcomes, an indicator might include a regular count of incidences of abuse, factual reporting on the increasing or decreasing distances that people feel able to move around, or health status reports which are known to be linked to protection needs. If your outcomes relate to legal obligations, indicators might include signs that IHL dissemination is now underway in an armed force and is increasingly understood and respected.

Protection indicators should be collected as consistently and regularly as possible so as to show trends and changes over time. A good indicator is not only illustrative of the outcome at which you are aiming; it must also be collectable and easily processed. What looks like the perfect indicator on paper will be useless in practice if it is too dangerous to collect the necessary information, or requires far too many hours of staff time to collate, process and interpret afterwards.

More qualitative indicators which require real listening and empathy to capture the subtleties of people's experience and their sense of security must be collected by highly sensitive staff members. Such monitors need to be carefully selected from within your staff. For example, it is unwise to assume that all national staff can naturally play this role because they speak the language and share the culture. As insiders to a society at war, they may well share the divisions or discriminations common to that conflict, and find themselves essentially out of sympathy with people of various groups and causes.

Wherever possible and appropriate, protection indicators are best chosen, collected and jointly interpreted in a participatory way with the civilian community itself – or those specially prioritised within it, such as young men, women or children. And where the responsible authorities are cooperative and engaged in protection, they too should be actively involved in monitoring.

Remember that there are four main types of protection outcome to be achieved:

1   **changes in the behaviour of perpetrators**, resulting in a reduction in the number of casualties, sexual violations, displacements, disappearances, threats and other measurable violations of human-rights and humanitarian law over time

2   **changes in the actions of responsible authorities and agencies**, resulting in the development and practical implementation of policies, commitments and actions to reduce violence, displacement and deprivation, and to increase civilian protection

3   **changes in the actions of people themselves** – which take the shape of improved organisation, mobilisation and political participation that enables them to avoid, resist or challenge the threats and policies against them so that they become protection actors and not simply the victims of violations

4   **changes in the daily lives of civilian communities**, resulting in increased personal safety, restored dignity, reduced vulnerability to threats, improved levels of health, wider freedom of movement and normal participation in livelihood activities, social networks and political life – this is the real bottom-line outcome that you seek.

With your precise outcomes in mind, it should be possible to choose a small number of indicators that will allow you to gauge over time whether your programme and its particular activities are having the intended effect.

Indicators can relate to **quantitative** and **qualitative** information. In other words, they can be 'hard' and count empirical data relating to incidents and conditions. Or, they can be softer and reflect trends in people's opinions, perceptions and the sense of their own safety. The information they produce can indicate positive, negative, mixed or paradoxical protection results (see below). A good indicator is also, like an objective, one that is **SMART (see Section 6 above, under Setting your objectives)**.

Once again, it may be useful at this point to return to the basic protection equation: **risk = threat + vulnerability × time** and to select indicators which relate to each part of the equation in your given context.

Capturing good and bad outcomes

Positive outcomes can be captured in the form of quantitative indicators, such as a reduced incidence of rape and a wider range of movement. Indicators can also be more qualitative, such as a reduced sense of fear, a growing sense of safety, recovered dignity and self-respect or an improved quality of dialogue between you and your interlocutors in the responsible authorities. These can all be detected by both informal observation and surveying. The same indicators might also be used to expose **negative outcomes** that would report a sustained or rising incidence of sexual violence and disappearance with increasing levels of fear.

The results of certain protection activities can also demonstrate **mixed outcomes**, which are often revealed in conflicting indicators. Following an increase in the government military presence in rural areas of Country K, for instance, quantitative indicators may show that the incidence of reported rape and abduction is greatly reduced but that women are still experiencing high levels of fear. This may suggest that women are threatened less by raids by armed groups than they are by potential sexual exploitation by increased numbers of government troops.

This kind of phenomenon is an example of the **protection paradox** whereby increased protection of one kind can render people vulnerable to new patterns of abuse – what we have called secondary risks. As seen above, these assistance-related risks can develop in relation to: relief resources that expose people to the danger of raiding; the collection of large numbers of people in protected areas that expose them to disease; or their flight to asylum in refugee camps which restrict their freedom of movement and render them vulnerable to exiled regimes and cross-border military operations. As much as possible, all types of outcome need to be anticipated, captured and analysed in your monitoring, and used to guide your protection work accordingly.

2 | 9

section **nine**

Principles of
best practice for
protection-focused
humanitarian work

The main approach presented in this guide to protection in humanitarian action can be summarised in eight key principles that can be used as a short *summary* for humanitarian agencies.

1 Focus on safety, dignity and integrity

The immediate protection challenge is to keep people physically safe, to preserve their personal dignity and provide for their wholeness as human beings. This is best done by working closely with people at risk and concentrating on safety, dignity and integrity as the protection edge of all humanitarian action. Remember the protection equation at all times: **risk = threat + vulnerability × time**.

2 Think about law, violation, rights and responsibilities

A protection approach means recognising that much civilian suffering in war is often the result of a *violation* of international law. It is this violation that then produces secondary needs. Civilians in war who are hungry, ill, injured, displaced, destitute and impoverished or who have been sexually abused are in a state of extreme need because their rights under international law have been violated. Their suffering and need often result from a deliberate *pattern of violations* that is integral to the policy and conduct of the war and is in breach of international humanitarian, human-rights or refugee law. Violations of legal rights impose clear humanitarian, military and political duties on governments, non-state actors and individuals.

3 Ensure respect

A protective approach requires that humanitarian workers go beyond an aid-only approach and also focus on ensuring respect for humanitarian and human-rights norms. This involves humanitarian agencies taking up some key skills and techniques that have been more explicitly developed in human-rights practice to date. These skills are vital if humanitarian agencies are to recognise and report violations, advocate more effectively, pressurise relevant authorities and adhere to international legal standards themselves.

4 Build on people's own self-protection capacity

Humanitarian common sense affirms the value of people's own knowledge, capacity, insight and innovation in any given situation that threatens them. As a result, good practice in humanitarian protection values close cooperation and participation in any relationship between humanitarian agencies and the people they are trying to help. People are seldom passive when they feel at risk: they engage in a range of finely judged actions to cope, respond, adapt and survive. This makes it essential that people are involved in, and often take the lead on, decisions concerning their own protection.

5 Work with clear protection outcomes and indicators

Have a clear sense of what daily life would be like if people were to be appropriately protected, and then develop specific protection outcomes as the guiding stars of your programme's objectives and activities. Devise illustrative and collectable protection indicators that provide the means of verification for your work.

6 Prioritise interagency complementarity

Different agencies have different mandates, protection priorities and expertise. They also work in different places and on different political levels, nationally and internationally. It is important to take advantage of these differences in regard to combined efforts to protect civilians in war. Where appropriate, precedence should be given to mandated agencies. Care needs to be taken not to compromise one another's protection strategies and activities at any of the three levels of protective action.

7 Prevent counter-protective programming or behaviour

Humanitarian agency staff can give, say and do things that seem sensible on one level, yet have a terrible effect on the very people they are trying to help. Instances of social and political insensitivity by international staff, and thoughtless programming, can pass unnoticed by agency staff concerned but can invite a terrible backlash against national staff and the community the agency is trying to assist. Similarly, an agency's relationships with key actors – including military forces, the international media and foreign governments – can be read in very different ways by different groups. Activities, attitude and behaviour can all prove counter-protective rather than protective, and must be constantly and carefully scrutinised to ensure that they do not expose individuals and the general affected population to even greater risk.

8 Be courageous but realistic about your agency's limits

Humanitarian agencies have relatively limited means with which to protect civilians. In many situations, mandated and non-mandated bodies lack the political authority, the military force and the legal mandate that would give them the practical power to protect civilians effectively. Recognition of this fact is critical to ensure realistic programming, to avoid excessive expectation and to preserve agency morale. Humanitarian fieldworkers are not the people primarily responsible for protecting civilians. While they must be as creative and courageous as possible in every situation, they are part of a much wider system of moral, legal and political responsibility. The tragic truth is that many efforts at humanitarian protection will fail. How agencies understand and deal with this is very important. More so than many other areas of humanitarian assistance, protective programming often has to operate with a sense of achievement that is as much about trying as succeeding. Often, it will not be humanly possible for humanitarian agencies to protect everyone. But where there is success, it must be valued deeply – even when it involves only a single person.

bibliography
and **annexes**

Bibliography

The following are publications and other resources that have been particularly useful in compiling this guide.

Anderson, MB (1999) *Do No Harm: How Aid Can Support Peace or War.* Boulder: Lynne Rienner.

Blaikie, P, et al (1994) *At Risk: Natural Hazards, People's Vulnerability and Disasters.* London: Routledge.

Bonard, P (1999) *Modes of Action used by Humanitarian Players: Criteria for Operational Complementarity.* Geneva: ICRC.

Bonwick, A. (forthcoming 2006) *Who Really Protects Civilians?* Oxford: Development in Practice, Oxfam.

Bouchet-Saulnier, F (2002) *The Practical Guide to Humanitarian Law.* Oxford: Rowman and Littlefield, in conjunction with Médicins Sans Frontières.

Carvezasio, Sylvie Giossi (2001) *Strengthening Protection in War: a Search for Professional Standards.* Geneva: ICRC.

Cuny, Fred (1999) *Famine, Conflict and Response: a Basic Guide.* West Hartford: Kumarian Press.

Darcy, J (1997) *Human Rights and International Legal Standards: What do Relief Agencies Need to Know?* Relief and Rehabilitation Network (RRN) Paper 19. London: Overseas Development Institute (ODI).

Frohardt, M, D Paul and L Minear (1999) *Protecting Human Rights: the Challenge to Humanitarian Organisations.* Occasional Paper 35. Providence, Rhode Island: Thomas J Watson Jr Institute for International Studies, Brown University.

ICRC (1983) *Basic Rules of the Geneva Conventions and their Additional Protocols.* Geneva: ICRC.

ICRC (2001) *Women Facing War.* Geneva: ICRC.

Inter-Agency Standing Committee (2002) *Growing the Sheltering Tree: Protecting Rights through Humanitarian Action, Programmes and Practices Gathered from the Field.* Geneva: Inter-Agency Standing Committee.

International Commission on Intervention and State Sovereignty (2001) *The Responsibility to Protect.* Ottawa: ICISS.

Mahony, Liam and Luis-Enrique Eguren (1997) *Unarmed Bodyguards: International Accompaniment for the Protection of Human Rights.* West Hartford: Kumarian Press.

Mancini-Griffoli, Deborah and Andre Picot (2004) *Humanitarian Negotiation: a Handbook for Securing Access, Assistance and Protection for Civilians in Armed Conflict.* Geneva: Centre for Humanitarian Dialogue.

Paul, D (1999) *Protection in Practice: Field Level Strategies for Protecting Civilians from Deliberate Harm.* RRN Paper 30. London: ODI.

Roche, C (1999) *Impact Assessment for Development Agencies: Learning to Value Change.* Oxford: Oxfam.

Schaufelberger, E and B Bernath (2004) *Monitoring Places of Detention: a Practical Guide.* Geneva: Association for the Prevention of Torture.

Slim, H (2003) 'Why Protect Civilians? Innocence, Immunity and Enmity in War' in *International Affairs* Vol 79, No 3, pp 481501.

UNHCR (1999) *Protecting Refugees: A Field Guide for NGOs.* Geneva: UNHCR.

UNCHR (2001) *United Nations Training Manual on Human Rights Monitoring.* Geneva: UNHCHR at <http://www.ohchr.org/english/about/publications/training.htm> especially Chapters vviii, x and xi, xii, xvi and xx.

UNHCR (2003) *Sexual and Gender-based Violence against Refugees, Returnees and Internally Displaced Persons: Guidelines for Prevention and Response.* Geneva: UNHCR.

Annex 1

International legal standards

The following is a list of key instruments of international law that relate to the protection of people in war. All agency staff members involved in humanitarian protection work will need to be familiar with them to differing degrees.

For full texts and key points about international humanitarian law, see the ICRC website at <www.icrc.org>; and for details of the texts and mechanisms of human-rights law, see the website of the Office for the High Commissioner for Human Rights at <www.unhchr.ch>. For information about the International Criminal Court, see <www.icc-cpi.int/home>.

International humanitarian law

- The Geneva Conventions of 1949 (especially the IV Convention on the Protection of Civilian Persons in Time of War and Common Article 3) and the two Additional Protocols of 1977.
- The Statute of the International Criminal Court.

International refugee law

- Convention on the Status of Refugees, 1951, and the Protocol Relating to the Status of Refugees, 1967.

International human-rights law

- Convention on the Prevention and Punishment of the Crime of Genocide, 1948.
- Universal Declaration of Human Rights, 1948.
- International Convention on the Elimination of All Forms of Racial Discrimination, 1965.
- International Covenant on Civil and Political Rights, 1966.
- International Covenant on Economic, Social and Cultural Rights, 1966.
- Convention on the Elimination of All Forms of Discrimination Against Women, 1979.
- Convention Against Torture and Other Cruel, Inhuman and Degrading Treatment or Punishment, 1984.
- Convention on the Rights of the Child, 1989.
- Guiding Principles on Internal Displacement, 1998.

United Nations Resolutions

- United Nations General Assembly Resolution 46/182/1991 Strengthening of the Coordination of Humanitarian Emergency Assistance of the United Nations.
- United Nations Security Council Resolution 1296 on the Protection of Civilians in Armed Conflict, S/RES/1296/2000.

Annex 2

Main points of UNOCHA's Aide Memoire for the Consideration of Issues Pertaining to the Protection of Civilians, 2004

1   Prioritise and support the immediate protection needs of displaced persons and civilians in host communities.

2   Facilitate safe and unimpeded access to vulnerable populations as the fundamental pre-requisite for humanitarian assistance and protection.

3   Maintain the humanitarian and civilian character of camps for refugees and internally displaced persons.

4   Ensure the safety and security of humanitarian, United Nations and associated personnel.

5   Facilitate the stabilisation and rehabilitation of communities.

6   End impunity for those responsible for serious violations of international humanitarian, human-rights and criminal law.

7   Build confidence and enhance stability through the promotion of truth and reconciliation.

8   Strengthen the capacity of local police and judicial systems to enforce law and order.

9   Achieve disarmament, demobilisation, reintegration and rehabilitation of former combatants.

10 Facilitate a secure environment for vulnerable populations and humanitarian personnel.

11 Address the problems of small arms and land mines.

12 Ensure the sensitisation of multinational forces to issues pertaining to the protection of civilians.

13 Address the specific needs of women for assistance and protection.

14 Strengthen the role of women as constructive actors in developing and implementing appropriate responses to protecting civilians.

15 Address the specific needs of children for assistance and protection.

16 Counter the occurrences of speech used to incite violence.

17 Promote and support accurate management of information on the conflict.

18 Address the impact of national natural-resource exploitation and illicit trade on the protection of civilians.

19 Minimise unintended adverse consequences of sanctions on the civilian population.